Patient Safe ..

Over the past decade or so, we have seen a multitude of improvement programmes and projects to improve the safety of patient care in healthcare. However, the full potential of these efforts and especially those that seek to address an entire system has not yet been reached. The current pandemic has made this more evident than ever.

We have tended to focus on problems in isolation, one harm at a time, and our efforts have been simplistic and myopic. If we are to save more lives and significantly reduce patient harm, we need to adopt a holistic, systematic approach that extends across cultural, technological, and procedural boundaries. *Patient Safety Now* is about the fact that it is time to care for everyone impacted by patient safety, how we need to take the time to care for everyone in a meaningful way and how hospitals need to enable staff time to care safely.

This book builds on the author's two previous books on patient safety. *Rethinking Patient Safety* talked about ways in which we need to rethink patient safety in healthcare and describes what we've learned over the last two decades. *Implementing Patient Safety* talked about what we can do differently and how we can use those lessons learned to improve the way in how we implement patient safety initiatives and encourage a culture of safety across a healthcare system. *Patient Safety Now* unites the concepts, theories and ideas of the previous two books with updated material and examples, including what has been learned by patient safety specialists during a pandemic.

Patient Safety Now provides the reader with a unique view of patient safety that looks beyond the traditional negative and retrospective approach to one that is proactive and recognizes the impact of conditions, behaviours and cultures that exist in healthcare on everyone. It is written not only for healthcare professionals and patient safety personnel, but for patients and their families who all want the same thing. Too often when things go wrong, relationships quickly become adversarial when in fact this can be avoided by recognizing that, rather than being in separate camps, there are shared needs and goals in relations to patient safety.

Patient Safety Now

Applying Concepts, Theories, and Ideas for Creating a Safe Environment

Suzette Woodward

Routledge
Taylor & Francis Group

A PRODUCTIVITY PRESS BOOK

First published 2023
by Routledge
605 Third Avenue, New York, NY 10158

and by Routledge
4 Park Square, Milton Park, Abingdon, Oxon, OX14 4RN

Routledge is an imprint of the Taylor & Francis Group, an informa business

ISBN: 978-1-032-01837-9 (hbk)
ISBN: 978-1-032-01832-4 (pbk)
ISBN: 978-1-003-18029-6 (ebk)

DOI: 10.4324/9781003180296

Typeset in Garamond
by Deanta Global Publishing Services, Chennai, India

Dedicated to Mum and Minnie

Forever in my heart

Contents

Acknowledgements...ix

About the Author xi

Introduction xiii

1 How Did We Get Here? 1
  What Is Safety-I?.. 1
  Policies and Procedures... 4
  Work-as-Done versus 6
  Workarounds..16
  Our Attitude to Error 18
  It Was 1980 Something 22
  Personalisation 27
  Expertise...32
  Teams 33
  Clinical Risk and Regulation...35
  There Is a Science to This! 40
  The 10%..42
  An Organisation with a Memory.......................................46
  Incident Reporting 54
  Incident Analysis and Investigation.................................61
  Global Challenges 72
  All Change...75
  Sign Up to Safety..76
  Still Not Safe 84

2 Where Do We Want to Be? **87**
What Is Safety-II?..87
Risk Resilience...89
Human Factors 90
Complex Adaptive Systems..................................93

3 How Do We Get There?..................................**103**
Safety-I and Safety-II.......................................103
Study the Mundane, the Ordinary 105
Learning from Excellence 111
Mind Your Language...113
Understanding the Impact of Incivility 117
Thinking about Culture 118
Investigating Differently.....................................120
Moving towards a Restorative Just Culture 121
Learning about a Psychologically Safe Environment 127
Implementing the Four Stages of Psychological Safety.......131
Improving How We Talk to Each Other 134
Schwartz Rounds...136
Drawing Lessons from Change Management 143
Caring for the People That Care....................................147
Learning from COVID-19..149

Conclusion **157**

References **161**

Index **165**

Acknowledgements

I would like to acknowledge the following people:

Bradley, my husband, who has always reminded me of the importance of saying 'please' and 'thank you'.

Steven Shorrock, who constantly amazes me with the way in which he is able to describe how we work so astonishingly well.

Erik Hollnagel, without whom this book would not exist.

Amy Edmondson and Timothy Clark and their brilliant work on psychological safety.

Sarah Garrett, David Naylor, and Chris Turner who have helped shape my thinking on safety-II, just culture, and incivility.

About the Author

Suzette Woodward has spent over 40 years working in healthcare, with the last 25 working in safety. She is a former paediatric intensive care nurse who is now an independent consultant specialist in safety and is a sought-after speaker at international and national conferences. She provides masterclasses and workshops on all aspects of safety.

In her career, Suzette has held Board-level posts at the National Patient Safety Agency and NHS Resolution, been a clinical advisor to the Department of Health and Social Care in England and (the former) Public Health England, and is a visiting professor in patient safety at Imperial College London and Northumbria University.

Academically, Suzette holds an MSc in clinical risk from University College London and a Professional Doctorate from Middlesex University and was the recipient of the Ken Goulding Prize for Professional Excellence in 2008. She was awarded an honorary DSc from University of West London in 2019.

Suzette was awarded the Daisy Ayris Medal for services to perioperative nursing in 2011, named one of the top 50 inspirational women in the NHS in 2013, one of the top 50 nurse leaders in the NHS in 2014, and one of the top clinical leaders in the NHS in 2014. Suzette has written two previous books on safety, *Rethinking Patient Safety* and *Implementing Patient Safety*.

Introduction

There comes a point where we need to stop just
pulling people out of the river. Some of us need to
go upstream and find out why they are falling in.

– Desmond Tutu

Wherever you work in healthcare and whatever role you have,
you will be wanting to ensure the safety of the patients in
your care. You will want to find ways of building safety within
your work. However, healthcare is an uncertain world and the
difference between safe care and unsafe care can be decided
in minutes. Over the last two decades and more, we have
tried hard to prevent things from going wrong, to detect them
quickly if they do, to limit the harm as much as possible, and
to learn for the future.

Today though, we are asking, *why are we not as safe as
we should be, given the amount of effort we have put into the
science of safety over the last two decades?* This question has
led to further questions about the approach we have taken in
healthcare and the tools we have used to date. Reflection and
critique of our approach to date by those that work in safety
have highlighted a number of misunderstandings and myths
but also a potential way forward. As a result, some have
asked, *why do we simply focus on the things that go wrong and*

why do we not focus on the times when we get it right in order to understand how safe we are?

Safety-I and safety-II has been coined by Erik Hollnagel. I was enthralled by this concept when I heard Hollnagel present it over five years ago now. I do not purport to be an expert but ever since I have been exploring with others what people think about it and how people think we could apply it to healthcare. During this time a few other concepts have grown in stature, such as restorative just culture and psychological safety, to name just two.

The goal of this book is to help the reader understand this new way of thinking about safety – safety-I and safety-II – together with these other emerging concepts. I hope it helps equip you with knowledge about the new ideas and practices that could help enhance people's ability to work safely. No matter what your job or role is at your workplace, I hope that you will find this book useful in helping raise awareness about the latest concepts but also to change the conversations, methods, and processes related to safety in your organisation.

It is written from the viewpoint of safety in the National Health Service (NHS) in England but hopefully will resonate wherever healthcare is provided. I have in the main deliberately used the word 'safety' throughout this book rather than 'patient safety' in order to reflect the importance of safety for both patients and staff.

Anyone who works in safety should not be made to feel that the work they have done to date has been a waste of time. This is not what this book is about, although it may not feel like that. I recall reading *Still Not Safe* and feeling guilty that I had been part of it all, that I had perpetuated the way in which we do safety. I had promoted incident reporting as the way to find and fix things, and I had promoted root cause analysis as a way to really find out the causes of incidents. I had made all kinds of things seem too easy to do – 'simply build a safety culture'. Easy. None of this is easy.

Where we are today has been built on all the learning we have done over the last two decades, none of which has been a waste of time. It has helped forge our understanding of what has worked and what hasn't, it has provided us with a depth of experience that will help us figure out what the future looks like. That's what learning is, it is emergent and clarified over time. Make sure that the new knowledge we gain is built on the old knowledge. The more we do things, the more we know, for better or worse. Value what you have done while thinking about where we can take safety into a different direction.

Part 1

How Did We Get Here?

What Is Safety-I?

Safety-I is defined by Professor Hollnagel as a *state where as few things as possible go wrong* (Hollnagel 2014). This is predominantly the way we do safety in healthcare today, trying to understand how safe we are through the lens of failure. This is a laudable but flawed approach. However, this is the philosophy that has laid the foundations and shaped everything about how we think about safety and how we do safety.

This philosophy mirrors society where in life we pay more attention to our failures and the negative things that happen to us. We pay more attention to the mistakes we make in life rather than our successes. The sad or negative events live long in our memories when the happy, positive ones can simply fade away. Consequently, negativity is considered more impactful than positivity. We are continually told that things are getting worse, that modern life is much more negative than our past. We pay attention to these stories and it leaves us longing for different times when it felt safer and kinder and more respectful. The media, for example, is particularly effective at pointing out where healthcare fails rather than where healthcare succeeds. Good news rarely sells newspapers.

DOI: 10.4324/9781003180296-1

The problem with getting caught up in the negative is that we put more weight on the negative problems and feel that the priority is to address the negative rather than the positive. For example, let's say I deliver a talk to ten people. In the feedback forms nine people said they loved it and one person said they hated it. What do I do? I stress about that one person; I want to know who they were and why they made that comment. If there is any detail associated with that feedback, I pour over it in detail. I almost ignore the other nine. Then I start to wonder if I should change the talk based on the tenth person's feedback, not thinking for once that I might in fact ruin it for the nine who liked it. Changing it might mean that the people who liked it might then not like it. This is also what we do in safety; we obsess about the times when things didn't go right and we wonder how we can change things. We don't consider whether the changes will impact on the times we get it right.

So, when we get that one negative comment, we feel we have to change ourselves to meet that one comment rather than accept that most people liked it so there is no need to change. Do you change things on a small number of comments or do you keep doing what the majority of people like? It is the same with safety; do you change things because of the small number of things that go wrong or do you keep doing what the majority of the system is doing, functioning OK?

We have always looked at safety from the negative point of view. Ever since I can recall, it has always been about the things we do wrong, the things we forget to do, and the things we should not have done. These have been termed as mistakes, errors, omissions, commissions, blunders, incidents, serious incidents, and never events. The terminology has confused the act with a name and has predominantly been viewed as things that humans do rather than the systems within which they work. We may never know the true level of failure or harm because events may not be reported or may go unnoticed.

This is the conundrum to those that want to constantly improve. Surely it is important to pay attention to the negative feedback in order to improve. There are some managers, coaches, and mentors who believe that it is important to point out people's flaws to help them grow. It has never worked for me. If someone points out my flaws, I will obsess about them and blow them out of proportion. I need honest feedback, but I would rather people pointed out what I did that worked. Deep down most of us know what our flaws are, do we really need others to point them out to us? OK, I hear you say, some people are not aware of what they do wrong and may be completely oblivious of their impact. In that case a kind word or two to highlight that would be a good idea but it has to be balanced. That person is not made up of flaws alone. Ensure that any feedback is balanced. Provide some feedback on things that you didn't like if you think it is really important and balance it with what you did like.

In safety we have tried to change all kinds of things based in the negative feedback – healthcare procedures, processes, tasks, equipment, practices, and even behaviours. We constantly look to the data that is providing us with the downsides of our work. As soon as I write that, I am nodding. Of course, we want to do that. A patient is unhappy, or an incident has occurred, or a staff member has been hurt – of course we should change what we do to prevent these things from happening. But what about the rest of the time? What is going on the whole of the time? Are these negative events a large or small percentage of what we do? What is it about them that can be or should be changed?

I am not sure we are very good at answering these questions, so instead we continue in a rather relentless fashion to capture the incidents via incident reporting systems and complaints processes. Analyse them using a causal methodology to 'find the root causes' to fix. Write a few recommendations for change. Job done.

What negativity perpetuates is unequal learning. It maintains that learning from failure is better than learning from success. Why is this the case? Is it because the failure is so painful for everyone both emotionally and physically? Is it because it is easy to see? Is it because this is how we have always done it? Is it because other high-risk industries have done the same?

In many other areas of life, we study the good in order to improve. Sports people study those who are doing well in order to replicate what they do. For example, in sports coaching those that are good at what they do are studied by others in the same sport with the aim of learning from their success. How did they run that fast, how did they row that well, how did they manage to hit the golf ball so far and so accurately? People want to learn from the best, those that are successful. Coaching is about inspiring the individual or team, building their confidence, and teaching them the skills they need in order to develop and work together successfully while ensuring they feel supported along the way. It relies on good communication and social skills, providing constructive feedback.

In healthcare, however, we don't shine a light on those that are brilliant at their jobs, those that others might want to emulate. Doing things brilliantly in healthcare is considered part of the day job. In safety we focus almost exclusively on the negative: what are the problems we need to address, what are the things we are doing that are going wrong. We design data collection systems, capturing incidents, accidents, never events, serious incidents, deaths, complaints, and claims. All of which are where we have failed. There is a desire to quantify the level of failure. How many patients are harmed? How many incidents are happening? What is the percentage? Is it getting worse or better? Are we less safe or safer?

Policies and Procedures

Directly linked to this way of thinking about safety is the view that what people do can be prescribed in some way: policies, procedural documents, guidelines, standards, and so on. This view asserts that all the people need to do is adhere to them and care will be delivered in the right way, by the right people and safely.

In safety-I the bad outcome is often attributed to the behaviour of the frontline staff. If they have been found to not comply with a rule or guidance or policy, then they are judged to have 'violated' that prescribed form of work. These are referred to in the safety world as violations. Violations are said to occur when healthcare practitioners are faced with situations in which they may need to take a risk. These are often referred to as violations because individuals or groups take action which is different from the expected standard or rules or procedures, i.e., they violated the policy.

People who commit violations are considered risky or reckless in their behaviour and are often threatened with sanctions. This adds to the fear of disclosing actually what happens in the everyday work, the workarounds they do, the guidance they don't follow. This fear silences people and they may either keep quiet or lie. This may lead to what people describe as the work-as-disclosed, i.e., people will only disclose what they think other people want to hear. Much can be learned by understanding why certain violations happen and why some become the norm. So, the response required is to pause before judging and to try to understand why.

There is often a huge difference between how the developers of these polices think and how the work is actually carried out. This is the difference between work-as-imagined and work-as-done. Why is this important? Because in safety people are held to account for these policies, when they may be unclear and unworkable.

We need to really consider our approach to policies. This is completely summed up by Dekker and Conklin (2022) (pp. 47–48):

> If the worker would simply follow the process nothing bad will happen, nothing bad could happen. That idea is crap. The idea that work is happening

the way work is imagined is overly simplistic. It denies the reality that the world of work is a world filled with uncertainty, variability, and constantly changing organizational priorities and operational goals. Performing work is not nearly as predictable as organizations desire work to be – and the act of wanting work to be predictable does not make the work stable or the statement true. Every worker, without fail every single worker, will tell you the work they do daily is different from the work the organization 'thinks' the workers are doing. Saying that every worker knows there is a difference between work as imagined and work as done is a bold statement. And yet, it is certain that this difference in work as done and work as imagined is real. It is vital information for the organization to capture, and important to recognize. There is a difference between the work being done in the way organization imagines that work being done, and actually doing work. This difference is normal and the better (and sooner) the organization understands and embraces this difference, the better the organization will function as an effective and reliable facility.

Work-as-Done versus ...

Over the last 15 years or so, the field of human factors has been introduced into healthcare. This has bought with it ways to describe the properties of work from a variety of angles. Understanding how we work in its many forms is helping us understand how this could then be improved. The two main areas of work that have been described are 'work-as-done' and 'work-as-imagined'.

Work-as-done is what people do to every day. In the main we are successful in our everyday work. This is because of our individual and collective expertise, our experience, and knowledge. We have an ability to adjust to the changes we face, to work around where we need to, and to adapt. This is within in an environment of multiple shifting goals, constant variables, continuous and often unpredictable demand. In healthcare it is rare that we can slow the demand down or prevent patients from coming in the door. Our work–is-done is impacted by limited resources (staffing, abilities, competency, equipment, procedures, and time) and a system of constraints, punishments, and incentives, which can all have unintended consequences. If you want to know how work is really done, ask the workers themselves. As Dekker and Conklin (2022 p. 50) say:

> The world's leading experts in how work is being done in your organization already are on your payroll. You have within the walls of your facility the opportunity to know all there is to know about how work is being done. This information is well within your grasp; all you must do is ask the workers to tell you how the work is being done.

In summary, on any normal day – a work-as-done day – people:

■ Adapt and adjust to actually demand and change their performance accordingly.
■ Deal with unintended consequences and unexpected situations.
■ Interpret policies and procedures and apply them to match the conditions and patients.
■ Detect and correct when something is about to go wrong and intervene to prevent it from happening.

Work-as-done is mostly impossible to prescribe, instruct, analyse, measure, or even simulate precisely. Yet when we don't comply, we are considered disobedient. This disobedience is then punished.

Work-as-imagined is what we imagine work is like or what we imagine the work could look like. The 'we' is often policymakers, standard settings, guideline developers, regulators, and commissioners. The term 'work–as-imagined' can often refer to the way people imagine what the work is like and set policy or design interventions for frontline staff to implement. However, there may be a considerable difference between what people are assumed or expected to do and what they actually do. If people who are responsible for developing guidelines or standards or policies and procedures are relying on what they imagine someone does rather than what the frontline workers actually do, then the policy could turn out to be unworkable, incomplete, or fundamentally wrong. If the designers think they have come up with something that 'will solve the problems at the frontline' and those who are at the frontline are left with the feeling that 'this doesn't solve our problems', it feels clumsy.

The incongruence makes it hard for frontline staff to implement things they are being told to do, resulting in frustration and workarounds. The unintended consequence of this is that it triggers a degree of fatigue in relation to initiatives that seem misaligned with the goals of their day-to-day work (work-as-done) creating a chasm between the leadership and frontline of organisations. When we fix the wrong thing for the wrong reason, the same problems continue to surface. It is costly and demoralising.

The creation of the gap between work-as-imagined and work-as-done is not intentional. There are many people who develop policies or safety solutions who do their very best to try to understand what is really happening on the frontline. They speak to staff and where possible observe the work in real time. It is also not all bad. Imagining things can mean a new way of doing the work that others have yet to think of; it can challenge the status quo and describe an ideal people may want to aspire to. However, imagining work on its own, in isolation of context, lived experience, 'work as one', can be risky and in some cases simply wrong.

Shorrock (2022) has taken this further and describes human work from multiple perspectives. I urge the reader to visit his blog website referenced at the end of the book. I provide a summary here.

Firstly, work-as-prescribed. In safety-I it is assumed that healthcare systems can be easily taken apart and that the elements or components of the system function are clear and can be described in detail. This assumption leads to detailed procedural documents or policies prescribing what people should do. There are hundreds if not thousands of them. Staff are expected to know them all and if these are not adhered to, the staff are held to account, even if they didn't know the policy existed, or they couldn't find it or couldn't follow it even if they knew it was there. An awful lot of policy documents are too long, too wordy, and unworkable in the real world.

Most work-as-done is carried out in areas of healthcare that are constantly adapting (ultra-adaptive) and consequently impossible to prescribe exactly. Not everything we do in ultra-adaptive environments (more on this later) can be written down in detail. In this case, the prescribed guidance is more likely to work if it is written in general terms rather than the fine detail.

Work as prescribed is usually the output of work as imagined. The written rules, standards, guidelines, protocols detailing how people should work. This can come from the Department of Health and Social Care, individual policymakers, the Care Quality Commission, professional regulators, royal colleges, other professional bodies, unions and other national organisations such as the National Institute for Clinical Excellence, or the NHS Resolution or the Health and Safety Executive. These form the way people are expected to work and are used to judge whether the work has been carried out in accordance with what they prescribe.

There are some specialties such as radiotherapy, chemotherapy, medication administration when the gap between work-as-prescribed and work-as-done needs to be as narrow as it possibly could be. This is where it is vital that the prescribed practice matches reality and is constantly reviewed to ensure that it remains so. However, we are falsely led to believe that we can describe all care in detail. If we did, we would be stifled by the constraints, we would not be able to adapt where necessary, and everything would take far too long.

Next, we have work as instructed, observed, measured, analysed, and simulated. Work-as-instructed is the way in which work is explained in order to support someone to carry out a task or procedure. It can be through work as prescribed (standards, checklists, etc.) but mainly relates to training or on-the-job instructions. Healthcare workers are more often instructed on the job rather than in the classroom. They are instructed by those more senior or more experienced than them to carry out a particular task or procedure, sometimes with supervision, sometimes not. In certain cultures, the instructions are not questioned even if people don't under-stand them or don't think they are correct or safe. Sometimes this can lead to harm both for staff and patients. Work as instructed needs to be supported by a culture that encourages people to question and challenge.

Work as observed is the attempt to monitor and observe what people do at work. It may be both formal and informal. It forms the input into work as analysed. Work as observed is often used by regulators or professional auditors and is linked to work as measured and work as analysed. In a complex adaptive system such as healthcare, it is not possible to observe all aspects of the work. This is because of the dynamic nature of the work, the variation of the work, the situations and circumstances of the work that is being undertaken, and the interdependencies that influence what is done.

With regard to research, work as observed may take the form of ethnographic study. These types of research are now being used to study work as done, in order to understand how practices are done well to support the safety-II approach. However, ethnography can be subjective depending upon the way the observer interprets what they see. In order to make the data collection and interpretation transparent, researchers attempt to be reflexive. This is the video reflexivity methodology. Reflexivity refers to the researcher's (observer) aim to explore the ways in which the researcher's involvement with a particular study could influence the research. Reflexivity also refers to the act of self-reference; the examination of an action or practice. A low level of reflexivity would result in individuals shaped largely by their environment. A high level of social reflexivity would be defined by individuals shaping their own environment.

Work as measured is the data that comes from work as observed which is then fed into work as analysed. In healthcare we are overwhelmed by the number of measures we are expected to capture and monitor. Shorrock sums it up for me in the following:

> In practice, work-as-measured is often to assumed to have more validity than it really does. It often does not measure what it claims to measure. Measures for aspects of work-as-done are also often overgeneralised, not evaluated properly in situ, or are affected by biases, especially when there are perceived or real adverse consequences for poor

measures (work-as-judged). Many aspects of work-as-done (especially work in the head, coordination, social behaviour) cannot be measured with high levels of fidelity. Quantitative measures can – via precision bias and false precision – appear to be more valid than they really are. Finally, work-as-measured can be affected by perceived and actual consequences, such as those associated with incentives and punishments, sometimes associated with performance targets, and limits. These may affect the selection, collection, analysis, interpretation, and evaluation of measures and associated data. A practical example is the four-hour target in UK hospitals, where accident and emergency (A&E) departments in the UK must admit, transfer or discharge patents within four hours. This has been associated with reductions in recorded waiting times, but also peaks just before the four-hour limit, and occasionally data falsification, without sustained improvements in patient care.

Work as analysed is the output of work as observed and analysed. It is the output of any review, inquiry, and audit. It is part of the examination of work-as-done: the scrutiny of what people do, by describing what people do from the facts and figures gathered. It is usually the work of expert analysts. Similar to work as observed, it is difficult to describe the nuances of everything we do in healthcare. It is constantly changing, there are multiple unseen interactions and unseen behaviours and pressures. For this reason, analysis can lose the depth of what we do and provides us simply with a surface view of what we do.

Work as simulated is usually conducted in simulation training where there is an attempt to understand how work is done but also to recreate aspects of care to try to see

how it was done at a certain time or can be used to test out
ways of working for the future. It is often used to support
team training or to support a particular skill that needs to
be practised in a safe way. It can be with work colleagues or
even with actors. There has been an increase in the use of
simulation training across healthcare and it provides a really
useful way of gaining experiential learning without the fear of
doing something stupid, or doing something wrong.

Work as simulated can inform work as imagined but will
still be different from work-as-done. In the same way as we all
change when we are being watched or filmed, we also change
or act or behave differently within the simulation space.

In order to know about any of the previous works. We
need to know what work-as-disclosed is. Work-as-disclosed is
the work we say we do or if we don't feel we can do that is
could be described as work as undisclosed. Work-as-disclosed
is how people describe what they do, either in writing or
when they talk to each other. This may not be the actual work
they do but the work they expect people to want to hear, the
work as it should be and not how it actually is. If there is a
culture of psychological safety where people feel safe to share,
then work as disclosed might be close to what people actually
do. As Shorrock says:

> What we do at work may be different to what we are
> prepared to say, especially to outsiders or 'outgroup'
> members. What a staff member says to a senior man-
> ager or auditor about work may be different to what
> really happens, for example. There are many reasons
> not to express how work is really done. But people
> will tend to modify or limit what they say about
> work-as-done based on imagined consequences. For
> instance, staff may fear that resources will be with-
> drawn, constraints may be put in place, sanctions
> may be enacted, or necessary margins or buffers will

be dispensed. So, secrecy around work-as-done may
serve to protect one's own or others' interests.

Don Norman (who wrote *The Design of Everyday Things* in
1988) was once asked by a computer company to evaluate a
new keyboard. He spent the day learning to use it and trying
it out on various problems. In this particular keyboard to enter
data it was necessary to differentiate between the 'return key'
and the 'enter key'. If the wrong key was pressed, the last few
minutes' work was irrevocably lost. He pointed this out to the
designer, explaining that he had made the error frequently and
that it was likely that others were making the same mistake.
The designer's initial reaction was to question Don on why
he made the error and why he didn't read the manual. The
designer then proceeded to provide Don with a detailed
explanation of the different functions of the two keys.

Don explained that he did indeed understand the two keys
but that he simply confused them. He told the designer that
they had similar functions and were located in similar loca-
tions. That a skilled typist would probably, as he had done, hit
the 'return' automatically without thought. The designer said
that no one else had raised this as an issue and the employees
had been using the system for months. Don and the designer
then went to talk to a few of them. He asked them if they
had ever hit the 'return key' instead of the 'enter key' which
resulted in them losing their work as a result. They said yes
and that it happened a lot.

Why didn't anyone say anything about it? They had been
encouraged to report any problems with the system. Don
considered that it was because it was considered a human
error. That the employees were happy to report when the
system wasn't working or there was a problem with the
technical aspects of the computer but when they themselves
pressed the wrong key, they assumed it was all down to

them. The employees felt they had simply been erroneous and would do better next time. This as you can see is a theme that runs through many incidents.

Therefore, for many reasons, work as disclosed may be only the partial truth. This may be because:

■ Explaining every little detail would be too tedious.
■ We do things automatically and we may forget some of the details when we come to explain it.
■ Depending upon who we trust, we may tailor it to the audience and when we come to explain what we do we simply say what we want people to hear or what we think they want to hear.

Work as disclosed is a particular issue for healthcare. In a culture of fear and when we are being scrutinised or investigated, we may 'just tell people what should or did happen not what does or did happen'. People often do not report workarounds, for example, and conceal the actual practices they do in order to keep patients safe because they are not what the policy says they should do. In that respect those designing safety interventions may think that the interventions are working when they are not because no one is disclosing that they are not. In order to learn from staff about their work-as-done and work-as-disclosed there is a need for both a psychologically safe environment and a restorative just culture.

And finally, we have work-as-judged. Work-as-judged relates to the way in which we are watched (work-as-observed), supervised (work-as-instructed), appraised, scrutinised, and investigated (work-as-analysed and work-as-measured). Work-as-judged relates to the judgement, evaluation, or appraisal of work and may be related to performance, competence, safety, and efficiency. Judgements are made based on what the work should be (work-as-imagined, work-as-prescribed) and compare it to the work as carried out (observed, measured and analysed, and disclosed). This applies to every single person who works in healthcare. We are judged by others and we judge ourselves.

When we are being judged we may act differently or say things that are different (work-as-disclosed) from our normal practice (work-as-done). If we are judged by people who are not from the same profession or people who lack an understanding of our area of work or expertise, then there is a risk that we will be judged wrongly.

People try to judge others in healthcare by looking at the standard by which they are supposed to act (work-as-prescribed) and assess as to how closely our actions were against this. This particular approach to judgement is predominant in clinical negligence cases. Judgement can also come in a number of ways from opinions of our colleagues, complaints or compliments, incident reports, investigations, and the media.

Work may be judged by anyone including the person under scrutiny or judgement. It requires people to agree what is acceptable and what isn't. This will change over time as society, expectations, knowledge, and expertise change. Judgement requires therefore those that are in judgement to be up to date, expert, and knowledgeable. They also need to be fair and as free as possible from bias.

Workarounds

One of the ways we try to maintain safety in our everyday work is to do a workaround. A workaround is a method for overcoming a problem or limitation in a way of working. Workarounds in healthcare are common, sometimes planned, sometimes not, but in the vast majority of occasions well meaning. A workaround is where individuals deviate from the prescribed work, often for genuine reasons. These are a few of the different types of workarounds:

- Erroneous or unintentional – the healthcare workers did not know the policy existed or that it had been updated or did not fully understand the policy and were not aware of the right steps to make.
- Routine — the healthcare workers routinely work around an unworkable policy.
- Situational or exceptional – the healthcare workers workaround the normal procedure to accommodate the situation.
- Optimising — the workaround is better than the prescribed way to workarounds and may be done to make the work more efficient, quicker, or even to maintain safety.

We don't have a clear understanding of the scale and nature of the workarounds because we don't study them and often staff don't feel able to disclose what they are doing. The workarounds become normal, the 'way we do things round here'. If the workaround is regarded as usual practice, then they are usually only detected when something goes wrong. Because of this, workarounds are intricately linked to when things go wrong and are considered the same as breaking the rules. Particularly in nursing and midwifery, they can lead to punishment, sanction, and professional retribution. But here's the thing. If most of the time work goes OK, if we believe in the 90% rule, then the workarounds must also contribute to things going right. Understanding why people don't follow policies is a key component of safety. The reasons may lead to valuable lessons for the organisation which may need to rewrite some of the standards or rules or may have to consider how these rules could be made easier to implement.

Our Attitude to Error

In safety-I there is a view that error is somehow preventable and that when people make mistakes all we need to do is tell them to stop making mistakes and possibly sanction them if they do. However, I know it is an obvious statement, but not everything we do will go right.

Imagine that you are in the midst of an intensive care unit surrounded by pumps, wires, and machines constantly flickering numbers and lights and you need to administer one drug in the patient's vein and one drug in the patient's nasogastric tube. By mistake you put the venous drug into the nasogastric tube and the nasogastric drug into the vein. Why did you do this? Maybe you were distracted, maybe you were thinking of the next thing you were going to do, maybe your brain said I need to put one of these in the vein and one of these in the nasogastric tube and I will put the first one I have in my hand in the vein, even though it is the one to sooth the stomach. Maybe the equipment allowed you to do so, it wasn't easy to see which syringe was for which and both fluids were the same amount and same colour.

When we realise what happened the people who are 'judging' are horrified. How could that happen? Was the person not paying proper attention, did they not care about what they were doing? This person is clearly incompetent or lazy. We have to stop this person doing this again and at the very least tell them off.

Because of the consequences in healthcare of mistakes and errors, we do need to try to figure out what happened in order to help design ways to prevent it from happening again. Solutions that help people get things right, such as the labelling or packaging of the drugs, or the connections between the syringes and the different tubing, or having someone checking what you do. At the same time, we still need to accept that this is part of life and work, part of being a human being who works in healthcare, and that we have made many mistakes before and will make many mistakes again in the future.

The term 'human error' makes a particular judgement. Human error clearly sets out that it is the human who is the cause of the problem and responsible for the outcome. In the main people use the term 'with good intent' to help people understand that human error is normal, i.e., we all make mistakes. But it implies that any failure, causal or contributory, is the fault of the human. In theory the term 'human error' relates to how human performance of a specific function might fail to reach its objectives rather than whether the human failed, but in practice the term misleads people to focus on error of the human. It implies that humans can be also fixed in some way; that the error is in some way controllable or a choice. It points to the individual rather than the system in which they work. By simplifying this as a cause, the solution to this is to stop the human from making the errors either by stopping them to continue or to restrict them in some way. However, we know that incorrect human actions at the frontline are due to a deeper set of symptoms within the system or the workplace.

Human error also stigmatises actions that could have been the right actions in slightly different circumstances. There is a fine line between the right and wrong actions which is often only determined when there is an end result or a known outcome. Human error is too often used to describe carelessness, laziness, or incompetence and is highly subject to outcome bias. What if we don't use the term 'human error' at all? Preferred terms are error on its own or performance variability, or erroneous conditions or system error. If all 'human activity is variable in that it is adjusted to the conditions' then the variability is a strength; indeed it is a necessity rather than a liability. As many say, failure is the flip side of success. By acknowledging that 'performance always varies and never is flawless, the need of a separate category for human error evaporates' (Hollnagel 2014).

This view that we can prevent errors is perpetuated by terms such as zero harm, zero events, or never events. The problem with seeking zero harm or never events is that they are impossible. There is a belief that if we count all the failures and we find all the causes of those failures and treat them that accidents and incidents are therefore preventable, this is termed the 'zero harm principle'. Zero harm is an attractive goal but unlikely to be achieved in any foreseeable timescale, if ever. The rhetoric of safety is one where there is a world in which no one is harmed in healthcare.

Never events in the UK are an output of this mentality in which there are a set number of events that are considered as 'events that should never happen'. Never events make safety language even more negative. Never events, is a similar term to zero harm in that it is a term used for a subset of incidents that are deemed preventable. They are defined as serious incidents that are wholly preventable, as guidance or safety recommendations that provide strong systemic protective barriers are available at a national level and should have been implemented by all healthcare providers. In the English healthcare system, there is a list of them. Once the type of harm is described as a never event then the goal is for the harm to never happen but because of the inevitability of error in complex adaptive systems they will happen. So, what happens is the leaders of organisations and frontline staff are then blamed when they do. This means that they are so fearful of reporting never events that they distort reporting and encourage underreporting of a never event. No one wants them to happen, but they do. If they are used to judge individuals, teams, or organisations, people will do their best to hide them. The opposite of never is ever or always and that in itself is as unachievable as 'never'. So perhaps instead of the terms 'never event' or 'zero harm', we should focus on the language that is 'achievable' or 'possible' or 'attainable'.

However, this view is also perpetuated from organisations such as the World Health Organization, the Patient Safety Movement in the US, and national organisations within the UK. Within the WHO ten-year strategy there are 35 specific strategies. Number one is the make zero avoidable harm to patients a state of mind and a rule of engagement in the planning and delivery of healthcare everywhere.

Even the WHO recognises that this is controversial, that opinions across global health about the wisdom of setting this kind of central or overarching goal are mixed. They describe it as a compelling vision. However, setting an unreachable goal is demoralising and demotivating and will not attract clinicians to its cause. The reason for the use of this goal, the WHO state, is that the narrative over the last 20 years hasn't worked so surely this is the direction that needs to be taken. The WHO claims that a reduction in the currently unacceptable levels of avoidable harm is entirely within reach. I would remind the reader that we don't actually know the true level of avoidable harm. We don't know if it is more that 10%, or is around 10% or less.

The actions they suggest in order to achieve zero harm is to recognise that safety is a priority, to have public commitment towards zero avoidable harm, to establish national safety programmes, map the existing policy and strategy landscapes related to themes such as surgical safety, medication safety, blood safety, and so on. Perpetuating the myth that safety is all about individual harms and also continuing the focus on acute care and not the continuum of care that patients experience. Additionally, they state that member states should, among other things, create national patient safety charters, participate in World Patient Safety Day and adapt WHO patient safety guidance, allocate adequate resources for patient safety implementation, and create minimum safety standards.

Improvers like to use 'stretch goals' and in this respect they would probably say that aiming for zero harm is a stretch goal and that there is nothing wrong with having this dream or aspiration. But we have to accept that a system can never be 'safe' it can only be as safe as possible. Healthcare is never about certainty; it is about the balance of probabilities and risk. It is filled with people who will make mistakes no matter how hard they try to be perfect. They are often working in systems that are not well designed or not designed to help people work safely and in conditions that increase the chances of things going wrong. If we tell them that we should aim for zero harm, then every time things don't go as planned they will feel like they are letting everyone down and that they have failed within an expectation that they should be perfect. We must not perpetuate the myth of zero harm because it assumes that all accidents or incidents have causes and if they can be identified it should therefore follow that they can be prevented and therefore they can be reduced to zero. This is an impossibility.

It Was 1980 Something

I along with everyone else who works in healthcare have made a number of mistakes. I have shared before the time when I was a staff nurse, when I was responsible for checking the drugs on the first drug round of the night on a busy paediatric intensive care unit and one of the patients received an overdose of a drug. We believe that it was ten times the dose, which is usually the result of a calculation error. A point I often make is that none of us can be absolutely certain what happened or what we did or where the error occurred. I recall when being interviewed at the end of the night shift and being asked, 'what happened'? and saying 'I don't know'. I don't know was not the answer I was supposed to give. I was supposed to be able to say exactly what I did wrong. I recall it all being a blur. One drug check after another. Anyone of the drugs I witnessed that night could have been the wrong drug. I believe I checked all the things I should check but clearly I didn't. What led to that mistake? Again, I don't know. Was it a calculation error? Was it a calculator error? Was it a dilution error? Still don't know. I can only assume (read guess).

It is one of the myths about safety. There is an assumption that if you look hard enough or ask the right questions, or ask enough questions, you will find the answer, you will find the root cause. I have investigated many incidents and believe me, sometimes you just don't know what happened. Sometimes it cannot be explained.

In my case all the clues pointed to the infusion being ten times the dose and it is highly likely from what we know about medication error. What we do know is that there are a lot of times when a calculation error is a key contributory factor to paediatric medication errors because for most children you need to calculate the right amount of drug depending upon their weight and in some cases the amount of fluid you need to dilute it in. Paediatric medications do not come in neat packages to deliver straight from the box.

What I now recognise is that part of the contributory factor towards the incidents was because we were using a workaround. We didn't call it that, we thought we were being really efficient. Our workaround was as follows:

> In paediatric intensive care there is usually one nurse per patient. At this time each of these nurses would draw up all the drugs for their patient in advance. The nurse in charge would then move from patient to patient checking the drugs laid out on the table at the base of the child's bed or cot.

Most of the time this way of working was successful. It was a workaround that worked. On this occasion it didn't. As mentioned earlier, one of the lessons we now know about workarounds is that a workaround on one day will work out ok and the same workaround on another day may not. It all depends upon the context and conditions that people are working under. For example, on one day there are no interruptions or distractions, on other days we would be interrupted and turn around to answer a query or the phone, our attention is distracted, our focus is disrupted. On some days we are alert and well rested, on other days we are fatigued or sleep deprived. None of us at the time were aware that these things could impact on our performance or our ability to work safely.

'In hindsight' is a phrase often used in safety. I know in hindsight that what we did wasn't good practice but it was our norm. This wasn't one or two of us that did this, it was all of us, we did this on every shift. As we know, our habits influence others and then they become rituals, customs, *'what we do around here'*, and before you know it, it is part of the system. It becomes our 'work-as-done', how we work.

In my case it was presumed that the incident was a result of sloppy practice and incompetence. There was no learning. We were told we needed to do better in the future. There was no investigation, no review that may have considered what happened and why. There were no changes to anyone's practice or the practice of the unit, everything simply carried on as before. We went back to work and carried on with the workaround. We continued as before because at the time we didn't recognise the link between the workaround or the distractions or the fatigue and the error that resulted. We just assumed it was down to us as humans, that we made the calculation error. Therefore, no changes needed, just us. We had to be more careful.

I don't recall having a language around 'things that went wrong' apart from talking about errors, complications, or side effects of the treatment. The only nod towards safety we had back then was forms that were kept on the nurses' station where we could document patient falls and medication errors. This was an early, very simple version of a risk management system. I would have filled out one of these forms which was then used as part of the meeting I had the next day with the senior nurse of the unit. That form was then placed on my personal record so that if I did another one it would be seen in light of this incident. I was told one incident will be on my file, a second one would incur sanctions, and a third one might mean I was reported to the Nursing and Midwifery Council, my regulatory body. Being reported to the nursing regulator was always used as a threat during my training.

At no point did we consider whether there had been any incidents like it before and importantly at no point did we put the incident into any perspective. I had probably either administered or checked thousands of medications prior to this incident and would go on to do the same in the future. Of all of those thousands, how many did I do successfully and how many did I fail to do in the right way? I will never know the exact number or the percentage but I do know that (based on medication safety research) my success rate would have significantly outweighed my failure rate.

Every now and then I google 'ten times the dose' and without fail there will be references and links to medication errors almost exactly like the one I was involved in. During one of these searches, I came across a story from 2011 that took my breath away. The story was about Kimberley Hiatt, a paediatric intensive care nurse in the US.

Kimberley was, just like me, a nurse who worked in PICU although her story was 20 years later. As a result of a 'ten times the dose incident', one of the children in her care died. A doctor instructed Kimberley to administer 140 milligrams of calcium chloride to her patient, a nine-month-old infant. She worked out the dosage in her head because she had administered calcium chloride hundreds of times. She in error miscalculated and drew up ten times the dose prescribed.

Similar to the incident I was involved in, a doctor noticed something was wrong. He noticed that the child's heart rate was increasing and a blood test showed a raise in the calcium levels. When she explained what she had done to another nurse they both realised the error. I read about Kimberley's interview for the investigation. She said she had messed up, that she was talking to someone while drawing it up and she told them that she would be more careful in the future. Almost immediately after the interview, Kimberley was escorted off the premises. I cannot imagine how that must have felt. From what we know about Kimberley is that she was not a bad person; she loved her job, she loved her patients. All of a sudden, she was isolated from the job, her colleagues, and the hospital where she had worked for over 24 years. We are told that she drove home panicking about what happened.

You can see she felt she was personally and solely culpable for this incident. She also gave us clues as to why the incident happened: distraction, automaticity, calculating in her head. 'I will be more careful in the future' is not a recommendation for sustained change. Four days later the child died and shortly after that Kimberley was fired. She struggled with the death of the patient and the loss of the career she loved. Sadly, she never got over this incident and seven months after she was walked off the premises, she committed suicide.

The changes made in the hospital rightly focused on preventing the incident from happening again. However, if the solution was to remove the nurse from the situation it's the wrong one; that does not lead to sustained change. There is one key lesson from this story – the hospital did not learn from the other tragedy that took place, the nurse's anxiety and subsequent suicide. In fact, in Kimberley's case, one of the employees said they felt that people were still afraid to admit their mistakes, based on what happened to Kimberley.

They suggested that people didn't admit mistakes because they were afraid of losing their jobs. It is vital in the memory of healthcare workers like Kimberley that healthcare providers take healthcare workers' grief seriously.

Personalisation

Because of our attitude to error there is a fear about it but also a feeling that it could be controlled in some way. Most of us think that if we have loads of experience and have practised something a lot or we really pay attention then we won't make a mistake. So, it is a shock when we do. When this happens, we do three things:

1. Personalisation – we think it is all our fault.
2. Pervasiveness – we think it is going to affect every bit of our lives.
3. Permanence – we think we are going to feel this bad forever.

In 2016 I came across a radio interview with Bob Ebeling. Bob was one of the engineers working on the shuttle Challenger 30 years ago – since the radio interview Bob has since died. This was his story. On 27 January 1986, Bob, the engineer, had joined four of his colleagues in trying to keep the space shuttle Challenger grounded. They argued for hours that the launch the next morning would be the coldest ever. Freezing temperatures (their data showed), stiffened rubber O-rings that keep burning rocket fuel from leaking out of the joints in the shuttle's boosters. For more than 30 years, Bob has carried the guilt of the Challenger explosion. He was an engineer and he knew the shuttle couldn't sustain the freezing temperatures. He warned his supervisors. He told his wife it was going to blow up. The next morning it did, just as he said it would, and seven astronauts died. Bob was simply not listened to.

Since that tragic day, Bob has blamed himself. He always wondered whether he could have done more. That day changed him. He became steeped in his own grief, despondent, and withdrawn. He quit his job. Bob, who is 89 now, spoke this year on National Public Radio (NPR), a radio station in the US, on the 30th anniversary of the Challenger explosion. If you listen to the recording, you can hear his voice; it is low, quiet, and heavy with sadness as recalled the day and described his three decades of guilt. 'I think that was one of the mistakes that God made', he said, 'He (God) shouldn't have picked me for the job. But next time I talk to him, I'm gonna ask him … "Why me? You picked a loser"'.

The listeners were so moved by this they sent hundreds of e-mails and letters of support to Bob. Engineering teachers said they would use him as an example of good ethical practice and other professionals wrote that because of his example they are more vigilant in their jobs. Allan McDonald, who was Bob's boss at the time, contacted him and told him that he had done everything he could have done to warn them; 'The decision was a collective decision made by all of us. You should not torture yourself with any assumed blame'. And NASA issued a statement commending courageous people like Bob who, they said, 'speak up so that our astronauts can safely carry out their missions'.

While this story relates to space travel, there are strong synergies with the way healthcare practitioners have across the centuries tried to speak out and not been listened to. If Bob had been listened to, he may have been able to prevent the death of seven astronauts. The similarities also with the way those affected by error live with the guilt and share for the rest of their lives, profoundly and forever affected by these events. We need to care for them, be kind to them, support them to come to terms with what happened and never be judgemental. Speaking from my own experience, the guilt never goes away but a kind word goes a very long way to help. Every healthcare facility should provide an after-event duty of care to all, a function that supports patients and their relatives and staff when things go wrong.

We need to help all of those people like Bob Ebeling. The people who are living with the guilt and shame and the people who are profoundly and forever affected by these events. It is my belief that they need to be cared for, that they need kindness not punishment and be supported to come to terms with what went on. Speaking from my own experience, the guilt never goes away but a kind word goes a very long way to help.

As we have seen how people can experience guilt, anxiety, depression, and more. They find themselves reliving the event days, weeks, months, and sometimes years later. They are often devastated and it can lead to their lives unravelling. Anecdotal evidence suggests that unsupported health workers may also change their place of work or leave and even some leave the career altogether. Well-trained, caring, experienced nurses and doctors are moving on, either to another hospital or another career altogether.

If people could talk to each other about these experiences, it would allow others to come forward to share with the rest of the group. That active communication should be encouraged but we lack the appropriate forums for this kind of discussion and there are no institutional mechanisms for helping the grieving process that all clinicians go through. Even if they are talked about at morbidity and mortality meetings, it is usually just to examine the facts and not the feelings of the people involved. In the absence of the mechanisms to help people talk to each other, people respond with anger and blame, or they may turn to substance abuse, give up their careers or even their lives.

For staff there is a fear like no other. Shock that can deeply affect the people involved. It becomes a whole world of blame. Incidents can lead to people being suspended, reassigned, or even fired. The way incidents are handled can means that staff simply want to leave.

An aspect of personalisation described earlier is that of personal competence. We have the notion that we can improve ourselves by carefully considering what we do and our judgements. And in doing so we make it all about ourselves. This onus of responsibility on the individual perpetuates the blame culture. Personal competence also fails to distinguish between the broader assessment of how we perform in general versus how we perform in the moment, thereby narrowing our judgement.

For patients, healthcare that once seemed routine and safe is now perceived as dangerous. There is a fear, a wariness, and loss of confidence in the healthcare system and the people who work within it, the people who are often still treating them. They don't disappear to be replaced with 'new improved versions'; they are the same doctor, nurse, physio, midwife, and so on. Patients still need care; staff still need to care. Sadly, often there is an almost immediate breakdown in relationships between the care provider and the receiver.

The problem with focusing on individual incompetence is that it misses a whole heap of learning about individual competence, collective competence of the team, and the competence of the system. We have been consumed with the idea of competence or incompetence for decades. Mistakes are thing you can prevent through being competent, experienced, skilful, and diligent.

Let us consider competence. Healthcare staff are trained for significant lengths of time to move from novices to experts. This training is a mixture of academia and experiential. Our competence is routinely assessed and our progress is dependent upon that competence. When things do not go as planned or when we make mistakes, we are considered incompetent. Sometimes even after one incident we can be labelled as incompetent and that label sticks. However, our competence is directly related to the conditions in which we are working. It is directly related to the personal factors I referred to earlier, our ability to function, our physical health, our mental health, and to the system factors such as staffing levels, access to expertise and support, the right resources and equipment.

It really isn't straightforward. We can also be individually competent but incompetent within a team. We can be individually incompetent but competent within a team.

Collective competence is a concept described by Dr Lorelei Lingard (2021). Lingard goes on to say:

- Competent individuals can come together to form an incompetent team.
- Individuals who perform competently in one team may not in another team.
- One incompetent member functionally impairs some teams, but not others.

She asserts that in healthcare there are many individual members of the team who are competent but when they come together as a team it does not guarantee a competent team. The factors that might relate to this include our ability or inability to communicate with others, our ability to speak up, or our deference to hierarchy. Collective competence is impacted by the complex system of activity in which people interact with each other and processes. Through methods such as briefing and debriefing, or huddles or handovers or interdisciplinary rounds, teams build competence and collective knowledge about how to work together.

As we will see later in the book, healthcare is a complex adaptive system. Therefore, our understanding of what helps us develop both individual and collective competence is vital for the success. Perhaps we need to move away from the goal or reliance on individual competence and recognise that healthcare today is far too complex to achieve this.

Expertise

Expertise and competence are intricately linked. What we currently have is the view that there is a hierarchy of expertise and that the person near, or at, the top is the person to go to for the answers to the most challenging problems. This is grounded in the concepts of novice to expert. Not every individual who progresses in the hierarchy achieves this ability to address the most challenging problems and neither should they. The true expert is one that recognises and acknowledges what they do know and what they don't.

Expertise is impacted by the tools, resources, and people available. Experts have to navigate their context to provide optimum care. There is also a need to accept a distributed level of expertise. A distributed approach does not deny the importance of the knowledge the expert brings to the situation but acknowledges the need to access additional expertise for any given situation. This is vital for complex adaptive environments and the dynamic nature of healthcare. The need for healthcare workers to be flexible, innovative, and adaptive is at the heart of safety-II and therefore we need to recognise that this requires a shared approach to problem-solving.

If I simplify things just for a moment. As we have mentioned, we have those that set policy or undertake research or create standards and then there are those that apply them. What we know is that there is a gap between the two. This can be described in a number of ways already explored in this book such as the gap between work-as-imagined and work-as-done. What is rarely talked about is the people that can help both the policymakers and the people doing the work. These don't really exist.

We have people who work in safety but they are predominantly people who collect data, support incident reporting systems, and undertake investigations. Some are involved in doing safety improvement. What we don't employ in healthcare are safety experts who are qualified in safety, can coach, mentor, and support those on the ground to understand both safety and how we can learn about our systems. This is partly because there are not many who would be classified as a safety expert in the same way that other high-risk industries do, partly because the expertise is not recognised as essential and partly a reluctance to fund such a role.

What we need is expert support, people who can provide wisdom. These are people with relationship-building skills, ability to manage team dynamics, and provide skilled facilitation.

Training on safety has been taken over by the technical methods. Training to undertake root cause analysis or a risk assessment, or use data collection tools. What it should be is about understanding what people's day-to-day safety feels like (work-as-done) and how the system could function better.

Teams

The way people work together is central to the safety of healthcare. Behaviours of individuals at all levels can play a role in the lead-up to incidents or in the prevention of incidents. Teams are people who are used to working with one another, often the same people. This is increasingly rare in healthcare where teams come together for a short period of time and then disperse. There are three key concepts in relation to teamwork that are important for the safety of patient care. The first is teaming, the second is individualism, and the third is collective competence.

We have known for decades that team work is necessary for delivering safer care. When people work well together, it can reduce the number of errors or incidents. There are almost no aspects of healthcare that are carried out by individuals acting alone. Most of our work requires people to communicate with each other and develop effective relationships, even if short. In our complex adaptive system, working in teams is dynamic, constantly changing depending upon the shift or the type of work. Amy Edmondson has described this form of team work as 'teaming'. Teaming is a verb that describes the art of communicating and coordinating with people across boundaries of all kinds, whether that be across profession, status, or geography. Teaming is needed more and more and in particular has been vital over the course of the pandemic with individuals being redeployed to different departments.

For people to be able to 'team' they need a sense of belonging – feeling accepted, included, respected, listened to, and fully involved. For teaming to be successful the purpose needs to be stipulated at the outset. It needs people to seek out everyone's opinion to build mutual understanding as part of the teaming to get work done. In safety we are concerned with making our complex adaptive system more reliable and less prone to error. Rene Amalberti has argued that the goal of an ultra-safe healthcare system is fundamentally constrained not by economics or science but by cultural values and system barriers. Amalberti and his colleagues say that we need to move away from individualism in healthcare and away from individual clinicians determining the degree of risk in their practice, from those that stress their own goals to the exclusion of others', and from those that embrace variation rather than standardisation. Amalberti often cites that of aviation, in that everyone who flies expects the pilot have the same competence as any other pilot and it should not matter who that pilot is. In healthcare it is asserted that there is too much variability of competence which means patients seek out different clinicians from others where they are able.

The question should not be whether a particular surgeon is performing well, but whether or not the system that is composed of the surgeon and all the other members of the healthcare team is performing well. It is the performance of that system, not the skills of any individual member of the team, that determines the success or not. Actually, in healthcare you want a bit of both. You want to combine individual skill with collective ways of seeing and working: the cognitive properties of individuals, plus the tools in the environment and the interactions of each member of the team.

Clinical Risk and Regulation

It was around 1992 when I started to wonder what I should do with my career. It was 13 years since I started my training and 10 years since I qualified. At the time, to progress in nursing, there were two main choices: to enter into academia and teach nursing or to take a role that related to management. This always meant that you had to move away from being a hands-on nurse. At the time I chose to manage, I applied for a role as a quality manager. This was someone who was responsible for auditing and improving healthcare processes. I thought at least I can use my clinical knowledge to help me in this new role.

In 1995, in the UK, an organisation called the NHS Litigation Authority (NHSLA) (now NHS Resolution) issued a set of risk management standards for all trusts (the term for hospitals and hospital groups in the UK). This was an attempt to reduce the number of clinical negligence claims by standardising a number of aspects related to clinical risk and reduce the chances of things going wrong in the first place. Like all standards they encouraged the promotion of good practice and covered a variety of areas of risk such as providing information, advice and consent, the use of healthcare records as well as induction, and training for staff and medication safety practices. The standards also included steps to develop incident reporting systems. At the same time there was an increased focus on regulation and the set-up of regulatory agencies such as the now Care Quality Commission (CQC) and the Medicines and Healthcare Products Regulatory Agency (MHRA). These have since grown over time and now every single healthcare and social care provider is required to adhere to the standards expected by these organisations and are assessed in order to demonstrate their level of compliance.

Regulation is clearly a means of monitoring and improving all aspects of healthcare. As an aside however, there is concern that regulation has got out of hand, that it is an ineffective form of improvement and creates a huge burden on healthcare providers. It has become, in the UK, highly bureaucratic and many are seeking simplification. In 2018, Oikonomou, Carthey, Macrae, and Vincent mapped the regulator landscape of healthcare. This revealed over 126 organisations who have some regulatory influence on NHS provider organisations. There are also in addition to this 211 Clinical Commissioning Groups. The majority of the 126 organisations set standards and collect data from provider organisations and a considerable number carry out investigations. The authors found:

> a multitude of overlapping functions and activities. The variability in approach and overlapping functions suggest that there is no overall integrated regulatory approach.

Back in the 1990s, as a result of the hospital joining the risk pooling system set up by the NHSLA I was asked to add clinical risk to my title and role. A clinical risk manager was a new role to the national health service (NHS) that every hospital was expected to have as part of the risk management insurance scheme. To be frank, I had no idea what that meant, but neither did anyone else. At least we had the standards we could use to help guide us. The standards were a clinical risk manager's instruction manual. We had no formal training or any specialist knowledge of clinical risk or risk management. It is hard to even recall that this was the time when there was no internet, no Google to ask.

Over the next year the NHS was filled with people like me who were responsible for clinical risk management, and who were unsure about what they should be doing. Our learning was on the job and from each other. I set up the London wide risk management group just to get a bit of peer support. We supported each other to implement the standards and to cope with the inevitable assessments undertaken by the NHSLS to judge how well we were doing. What was interesting to me was that this was my first recognition that healthcare was risky and that we could try to work out what risks we could prevent and how we could minimise the impact of those risks.

In the beginning I was full of enthusiasm. I followed the standards and set up an incident reporting system. Collected the paper forms and tried to learn from them. The team grew. Five years later I move from a shared office with the complaints and claims managers to an office of my own – I needed the room for the number of filing cabinets. Filing cabinets full of incident reports. I was drowning. I didn't know what to do with them. I counted them, created lovely colourful graphs of things going up (never down). I tried to turn them into themes and build the patterns, listen to what the data was telling me. I realised it was so much harder to do than I initially thought.

Sadly, the whole thing was focused individuals and their performance. And the people, the frontline clinicians in particular, were frightened of us, terrified of us. I had a team by then and we would walk onto the wards and people would do anything to get away from us, walk away, look the other way, get busy. To others we represented the potential for their careers to be ended. Some of the reports led to investigations, usually triggered by a complaint or claim rather than the actual incident. I have to say I don't recall providing any support to anyone, my focus was on getting the information and doing my job and that did not include helping people cope with the impact of the incident or the investigation that followed. I collected the statements, heard the stories, talked to the families, promised things would be different. Yet, despite this, the same things kept happening.

Our approach to risk can shift depending upon the pressures and circumstances we are in, for example we can shift from being risk averse to a risk taker depending upon what pressures we are under. This can shift us from working safely to being riskier and then potentially reckless. This situation may become normalised. An example often used is driving. We all know in the UK we are supposed to drive on motorways (freeways) at a maximum speed of 70 miles per hour, but occasionally people shift into a risky speed of around 70–75 (described as 'illegal normal') but then even more rarely people may increase their risky behaviour by driving at around 80 miles per hour, and in some very minor occurrences some people may go much higher than this (illegal-illegal). We shift our behaviour because of demand, external pressures, individual and social forces. If we are late for an appointment, or if our partner is in labour, we are highly likely to drive must faster than usual. This could occur to most of us at one time or the other. However, people that are reckless are smaller in number. In healthcare Amalberti suggests it is likely to be between less than 1% and 5% of people who take extreme risks, or are reckless in their behaviour.

Systems *of* thinking relates our approach to risk and decision-making (Kahneman 2011). It is argued that there are two systems of thinking that people are engaged in through the course of their daily activities.

1. System 1 - automatic, intuitive, effortless, nonanalytic.
2. System 2 - effortful, analytic, creative, deliberative.

Automatic thought processes come into play when we are driving a familiar route. We feel like we almost got there on automatic pilot. Effortful thought processes come into play when we drive to a new destination and there is a choice of routes, some of which may be better at different times of day and may depend on traffic and so on. Choosing the best route requires deliberation and effort.

In the context of healthcare, system 1 and system 2 have been viewed as being based on tacit and explicit knowledge respectively. Tacit knowledge are the skills, values, and experiences learned during observation and practice that are not explicitly stated or known to practitioners, whereas explicit knowledge is the conscious application of defined rules and objectively verifiable data to the patient's problem, such as evidence-based guidelines.

According to automaticity theorists, individuals move from system 2 (requiring attention, effortful) to system 1 (automatic, intuitive) as they gain experience. An experienced nurse taking a patient's blood pressure simply and effortlessly puts the cuff around the arm and takes the blood pressure while talking with the patient simultaneously, a task that would have required much more of her attention when the task was new. As we become experienced in an activity, whether it is a physical task such as taking a blood pressure or a mental task such as the diagnosis of a skin rash, the effort that is required to perform that task diminishes over time. The expert simply knows (or thinks they know) what to do and how to do it.

Many errors committed by experienced clinicians can be due to their overreliance on the automatic way of working, and overreliance on the automatic mode is termed as drifting. Surgeons describe the fact that can they make errors during the routine, easy, or boring parts of the procedure where they felt they had drifted off. Routine cases or times of boredom can lead to people not paying as much attention as they should; they end up by being distracted by their own mind or by others.

I knew I needed to know more if I was going to be any good at this or I should go back to being a paediatric intensive care nurse. Luckily for me one of the first academic courses related to clinical risk had just been commissioned. So just a few years later I found myself studying an MSc in Clinical Risk at University College Hospital, run by Charles Vincent and Pippa Bark.

There Is a Science to This!

The MSc was a revelation. What I didn't expect to happen was how much I would love it. I wanted to find out everything I could about clinical risk. This was one of the best things I could have done. I was thrust into a world of new information and new thinking. I learnt about healthcare research in relation to patient harm. I learnt about of the first studies carried out in 1974 in California, in the US, and published in 1977 where the researchers found that out of total of three million hospital admissions, around 5% (140,000) of them resulted in injuries, with just under 1% (24,000) of them due to negligence. I learnt about a later study in 1992, the Utah and Colorado study, estimated that as many as 98,000 patients in hospital settings in the US died each year as a result of problems related to their care. All of this was eye opening to say the least.

One of the key things I took from during my time on the MSc was that asking clinicians to try harder or to stop making mistakes was not the answer. For example, we studied the work of James Reason and read his book *Human Error* (1990). James Reason described human error is the inadvertent action of doing something wrong; something that was not what it should have been done, a slip, a lapse, a mistake. He reminded us that we all make mistakes all of the time; like picking up the wrong keys, forgetting your ID, miscalculating

a medication dose, missing a turnoff from the motorway,
picking up strawberry yoghurt instead of raspberry, calling our
children by the wrong names. He asserted that most of the
errors that we make every day have minimal consequences. In
healthcare however, sometimes even small errors can have the
potential for dire consequences.

We studied the work of Don Norman, who wrote *The
Design of Everyday Things* (1988), which described the
potential for error from poor design. In my view it is a much
underused book written well before its time. For me he
described a way of looking at safety that was exciting and
inspiring. That you could potentially design equipment, or
processes that would make it impossible (or certainly less
likely) to do the wrong thing. We have been searching for
these design solutions ever since. I came away from the course
with the desire to do things differently. To stop punishing
individuals for their errors, since almost all of them were
beyond their control, and to work out how we can change the
faulty systems that 'set them up' to make mistakes. I wanted to
see how we could design errors out of the system.

We learnt that anaesthesiologists were the first to truly
embrace the concepts of patient safety. They undertook a
study in the late 1970s reviewing systems failures and recommended solutions such as alarms for airway disconnection.
During the 1980s, anaesthetists became the leading specialty
to address the safety of patient care. This work significantly
reduced the risks associated with an anaesthesia which even
today is one of the safer aspects of patient care as a result.
Anaesthesiologists held symposiums on deaths and injuries as
well as forming the US group, the Anesthesia Patient Safety
Foundation (APSF), in 1984. This interestingly, may well be the
first use of the term patient safety. In 1989, in Australia, the
Australian Patient Safety Foundation was founded in order to
capture anaesthetic events and errors. These efforts were dramatically successful: they reduced the mortality of anaesthesia

by 90%, from 1 in 20,000 to 1 in 200,000, within a decade. They were the first specialty to use simulation training to help people manage critical events. The use of simulators has now been expanded throughout all of healthcare.

We heard about the pioneers of safety, Jens Rasmussen, James Reason, Lucian Leape, and Don Berwick, and, of course, Charles Vincent. Lucian Leape, for example, was one of the first people to call for cultural change and to clearly state that even the best people make mistakes, even the most conscientious clinician had the potential to be erroneous. All of us in safety have followed these thinkers and we owe them a great debt of gratitude.

The 10%

During the MSc I was invited to shadow research nurses of one particular study in the UK and to review a few case notes. Little did I know that I was helping in a study that is now considered the seminal piece of research in the UK to assess the level of harm in healthcare. This study was published by Charles Vincent and colleagues (2001) which estimated that just over 10% of patients suffered harm in hospitals caused by a range of errors or adverse events in the course of receiving hospital care of which around half of them were preventable. The study was carried out at two acute hospitals in the London area. The following is from a summary of the study.

> The team (including me for one or two days) reviewed 500 randomly drawn records from site 1 between July and September 1999 and 514 records from site 2 between December 1999 and February 2000. They reviewed 273 (26.9%) records from general medicine (including geriatrics), 290 (28.6%) from general surgery, 277 (27.3%) from orthopaedic

surgery, and 174 (17.2%) from obstetrics. Admissions to the four specialties studied in 1998-9 were 19397 in site 1 and 18335 in site 2. The proportions of admissions studied were 2.6% and 2.8% respectively.

The team consisted of an experienced nurse who worked as project manager with four part time research nurses. A consultant physician acted as lead medical assessor, working with five part time surgical and obstetric colleagues, each of whom had been qualified for a minimum of 10 years. Each reviewer screened sets of notes under supervision until they were judged to be fully conversant with the review process.

The nurse reviewers used 18 predefined screening criteria to assess the case records. Records that screened positive (n = 405) were then reviewed by clinicians, who identified any adverse events and completed a detailed questionnaire. The clinicians assessed the impact of each adverse event on the patient in terms of disability and additional bed days, likely cause, place and date of occurrence, type of adverse event (for example, whether related to a particular procedure or treatment), and preventability and recorded detailed clinical information. Records were reviewed once only, although difficult issues were resolved after duplicate review and discussion between two or more assessors. The study was small and based on only two hospitals with a case mix that did not accurately reflect all of hospital practice. The specialties included in the review could have had higher rates of adverse events than other specialties.

The results were that out of a total of 1014 patients, 110 (10.8%) experienced an adverse event. However, some patients experienced multiple events, and the overall number of events was 119 (11.7%).

There was no significant difference in sex between patients who did and did not experience an adverse event. However, patients with adverse events were older than those who did not experience an adverse event. Seventy-three (66%) patients who suffered an adverse event had minimal impairment or recovered within one month; 37 (34%) patients developed an injury or complication that resulted in moderate impairment (21 patients; 19%) or permanent impairment (seven patients; 6%) or contributed to death (nine patients; 8%). Overall, 53 (48%) adverse events were judged preventable.

The study concluded that 10.8% of patients admitted to hospital experience an adverse event, with an overall 11.7% rate of adverse events when multiple adverse events are included. About half of these events were judged preventable. Therefore, around 5% of the 8.5 million patients admitted to hospitals in England and Wales each year experience preventable adverse events, leading to an additional three million bed days. The total cost to the NHS of these adverse events in extra bed days alone would be around £1bn a year.

A third of adverse events led to moderate or greater disability or death. Some adverse events were considered serious and traumatic for both staff and patients. There were frequent, minor events that often go unnoticed in routine clinical care and yet can have massive economic consequences.

As you can see it was an extensive care note review but despite that it was still only a review of acute care in one geographical location so one could ask how much of it can be extrapolated to represent the whole of healthcare. The answer is that it can't and yet the statistic has stuck. The statistic of

10% is used everywhere, certainly in the UK. To this day it is used in political speeches, policy documents, books and articles. It is a neat number. It is not the true number because we don't know what that is, but it is something to go on. To be fair there may never be a perfect answer, as no one knows how many people are harmed by their care, but everyone agrees that it needs addressing. Whether the number is more or less right or even a little bit wrong it tells us something.

The study had been triggered by the Harvard Medical Practice Study (1991). This had started out as a way to understand the scale of the problem in respect of negligence cases. A group of doctors in the US had carried out a study of patient records. The team studied 30,000 randomly selected discharge records from 51 New York hospitals in the United States. What they noticed however was that the patient records included adverse events of patients being harmed by errors made during their stay. Some of these errors were felt to be preventable. They found that serious adverse events (harm related to the care provided and not their illness or disease) occurred in 3.7% of the patients in their study. Of the 3.7% adverse events, the researchers considered that 58% were attributable to error and deemed preventable and 13.6% had resulted in death.

The Harvard Medical Practice Study methodology was to use retrospective case note review. This study has been replicated and adapted in terms of its methodology across the globe including in the study in the UK. The results of these studies have identified incidence of adverse event rates, across a variety of countries, ranging from 2.9% to 16.6% of all hospital admissions and those deemed preventable ranging from 1.0% to 8.6%.

Retrospective case notes reviews have their fair share of critics. We know they only provide a snapshot of a particular episode of care, and a particular time and place and that the opinions of reviewers are subjective. There is subjectivity in relation to differing views of life expectancy, preventability and the quality of care. For example, preventability is usually measured on a 1 to 6 Likert scale with preventable deaths defined as those scoring 4 and above. Reviewers find it difficult to agree on these measures. Issues also include the poor quality of the records themselves, the hindsight and the many other biases that affect judgement, and the fact that the record reviews are predominantly from acute care only.

An Organisation with a Memory

In many ways the year 2000 was the start of the safety movement as we know it today. In that year a report was published by the Chief Medical Officer Sir Liam Donaldson, published *'an organisation with a memory'* after convening a group of safety experts, including James Reason, to understand what we needed to do to reduce the incidence of harm in the NHS.

In the preceding years there had been an investigation into high mortality of children receiving cardiac surgery in the Bristol Royal Infirmary. So, when Sir Liam Donaldson was appointed as Chief Medical Officer, he was instrumental in bringing the issues of safety to the forefront. He had read the work of James Reason and other human factors experts and wanted to understand how these could be applied to healthcare. Just two years after his appointment, the Department of Health published *An Organisation with a Memory* (2000).

The publication provided a platform for the data from a number of research studies including the now called 'Vincent study' in acute care. It talked about how there were things going wrong in healthcare that could be prevented, incidents in surgery, maternity, medication processes and so on.

At the time NHS reporting and information systems provided patchy and incomplete data related to the scale and nature of the problem of failures in healthcare so the report was a mixture of data collected and data estimated. The publication stated that every year:

- Four hundred people died or were seriously injured in adverse events involving medical devices.
- Nearly 10,000 people reported to have experienced serious adverse reactions to drugs.
- Around 1,150 people who had been in recent contact with mental health services committed suicide.
- Nearly 28,000 written complaints were made about aspects of clinical treatment in hospitals.
- Hospital acquired infections – around 15% of which were considered avoidable – were estimated to cost the NHS nearly £1 billion.

The NHS during this time was paying out around £400 million a year settlement of clinical negligence claims, and has a potential liability of around £2.4 billion for existing and expected claims. This figure has continued to rise year on year. In 2020 the number had increased to a potential liability of £4.3 billion.

An Organisation with a Memory cited two lessons from the experience of other high-risk industries:

1. Organisational culture – This was considered central to every stage of the learning process, from ensuring that incidents are identified and reported through to embedding the necessary changes deeply into practice. There was evidence that a safety cultures, where reporting is encouraged, can have a positive and quantifiable impact on the performance of organisations. A blame culture on the other hand was thought to lead to a cover up of errors for fear of retribution. A blame culture would lead to a failure to identify the causes of

failure, because of the focus on individual actions rather than the role of underlying systems.

2. Reporting systems – It was considered that reporting systems were vital in providing a core of information on which to base analysis and recommendations. Experience in other industries demonstrated the value of systematic approaches to recording and reporting of adverse events and near misses.

The report concluded that the NHS failed to learn the lessons from when things go wrong and recommended a fundamental rethink in the way the NHS approached learning from incidents. There were four main areas that needed addressing:

1. Unified reporting mechanisms for when things go wrong.
2. A more open culture.
3. Mechanisms for putting lessons learned into practice.
4. An appreciation of the value of the 'system approach' to learning from errors.

Following the publication, the NHS hosted its first national conference on patient safety. It coincided with the publication of a special BMJ issue on patient safety that I still have today. For many, including myself, this was a defining moment.

As I have mentioned, prior to the year 2000 the science of safety was relatively non-existent. There are undoubtedly many unsung and unpublished individuals who have noticed aspects of poor safety and attempted to change behaviour and practice in order to minimise harm to patients but literature searches relating to patient safety reveal very little until we reach the 1980s. The science of safety as we know it today grew substantially from this time. Our knowledge and awareness related to safety rose exponentially and there was no going back.

In the UK, as a result of *An Organisation with a Memory*, a new organisation was set up to oversee the safety of patients in England and Wales, called the National Patient Safety Agency (NPSA). The Agency designed the National Reporting and Learning System and captured incidents from every area of healthcare, acute care, mental health, primary care, community and ambulance services.

It was launched in 2001 and in 2003 I was employee number 53. We had the most amazing opportunity to make a massive difference to the way safety was approached in the NHS and to reducing harm across the system. One of the NPSA's objective was to promote an open and fair culture in hospitals and across the health service, encouraging doctors and other staff to report incidents and near misses. It was made clear that the purpose of reporting was to enable healthcare providers to learn lessons from each other in order to improve safety, not to identify individuals or organisations to punish.

Some of the most exciting stuff the NPSA did was look at the design of equipment and medications. A number of medications were and still are packaged in the same way. Liquids are often put in glass vials with similar labels, such as solutions for sodium chloride (relatively harmless) and potassium chloride (potentially lethal). Mix these two up and a patient could die. So, the Agency worked with the pharmaceutical industry to try to improve the naming and packaging of drugs. There were too many that sounded alike and too many that looked alike.

We looked to colleagues in aviation and air traffic control and promoted the models that had been identified by *an organisation with a memory* such as incident reporting, root cause analysis and the use of checklists. We also looked to the US healthcare system. They had set up a similar organisation called the National Patient Safety Foundation. I recall attending one of their conferences in Washington and being amazed at the conversations that were being held. They were talking about creating a culture of safety, they described solutions to medication error and importantly they talked about the human cost both to patients and the people who care for them. There were moving patient stories that left us with a burning passion to do all we can to prevent another story like the one we had heard.

In early 2003 when I joined the National Patient Safety Agency a group of us pulled together the latest thinking on safety and wrote national guidance for the NHS, titled *Seven Steps to Patient Safety* (2003). In the early days of safety many of us fell into the trap of disseminating guidance and expecting change to happen simply as a result, but after a while we have been forced to admit that things didn't turn out as we had originally intended and planned. A significant effort went into producing the guidance which was based on a combination of a systematic review of the research, assimilation of the international and national safety knowledge and understanding, together with personal experience and expertise. We consulted people on the frontline and we sought help in writing the guidance so that it was easy to understand and interpret. Seven Steps was launched at the NPSA's annual conference in 2004 and a copy disseminated to every healthcare facility throughout the NHS by NPSA staff. The seven steps which were at the heart of the guidance were also used as the basis for training of over 8,000 NHS staff in safety. Over the following five years, the seven steps were adapted for primary care and community care settings. It was adopted by countries as far as Hong Kong as a way to develop a safety framework.

The Agency delivered nationwide training, set up annual conferences, launched interventions such as Clean Your Hands, Matching Michigan, and Patient Safety First.

Clean Your Hands was linked to a WHO global campaign on hand hygiene. While the evidence base for washing hands or using hand sanitiser before touching a patient was strong, compliance was weak. In fact, the last two years of a global pandemic has shifted the world's attention towards the importance of hand washing in a way we could only have dreamt of. Clean your hands campaign was extremely successful in raising awareness of the importance of hand hygiene and improving practice. As a result of the campaign all healthcare settings placed hand sanitiser throughout their organisations.

Matching Michigan was an initiative to reduce central line infections. The aim was to match the work of Peter Pronovost and Christine Goeschel. They had been able to significantly reduce central line infections across the Michigan Hospital and Healthcare Association. They recruited 127 hospitals across the state. Ninety-six of them completed the initiative and reduced the number of infections, over half of the hospitals were able to get their infection rates to zero. While the NPSA was unable to match Michigan they did succeed in reducing the infection rate in central line infections. Mary Dixon-Woods and colleagues (2013) later carried out an analysis of how the Michigan collaborative had been so successful. The researchers concluded that five features were crucial to its success:

1. Social pressure among state's ICUs to participate – as the programme got underway, ICU leaders didn't want to be left out.
2. Creation of a network community with coaching, and workshops, and data.
3. Inclusivity of all stakeholders with a vertically integrated programme structure.
4. Use of data on infection rates to rank units' performance.
5. Use of coercive measures, by programme leaders, such as contacting hospital CEO s to ask for data and asking ICUs to withdraw from the programme if the data were not forthcoming.

One of the campaigns launched by the NPSA was *Patient Safety First.* This endeavoured to use lessons from the Institute for Healthcare Improvement (IHI) and its 100,000 Lives Campaign. IHI set a goal of saving 100,000 lives and called on healthcare organisations to implement six specific healthcare interventions: rapid response teams, medication reconciliation, immediate revascularisation for myocardial infarction, reducing central line infections, ventilator associated pneumonia, and the use of perioperative antibiotics. Patient safety first also used lessons from the Clean Your Hands Campaign (NPSA), the Safer Patients Initiative (Health Foundation UK), Operation Life (Denmark), Safer Healthcare Now (Canada), and the World Health Organisation Global Safety Challenges.

Safety is an extensive and complex subject, with implications in every single aspect of healthcare. In order to create a campaign that was both meaningful and measurable, Patient Safety First focused on five interventions that were deemed to have a significant impact on care.

1. Leadership for safety – a compulsory action for all trusts signing up to the campaign was to implement the leadership intervention. It focused on getting Boards fully engaged with safety by demonstrating that it is their highest priority.
2. Reducing harm from deterioration – by reducing in-hospital cardiac arrest and mortality through early recognition and treatment of the deteriorating patient.
3. Reducing harm in critical care – by reducing central line infections and ventilator associated pneumonia.
4. Reducing harm in perioperative care – by reducing surgical site infections and implementation of the World Health Organisation's Surgical Safety Checklist.
5. Reducing harm from high-risk medicines – by reducing harm associated with anticoagulants, injectable sedatives, opiates, and insulin.

All trusts were asked to participate in the leadership intervention to help Boards become more engaged with safety. They could then choose anything from one to all of the four clinical interventions. The interventions were chosen because of their importance in terms of prevalence for high risk and harm. The National Reporting and Learning System incident data provided the evidence base. There was already published evidence in relation to the solutions that could be implemented and the benefits could be easily articulated.

The implementation principle was to support existing activity and not add new initiatives to the system where possible. Messaging and action were aligned with other safety work across the NHS including the NPSA alerts and solutions, Department of Health Guidance, and training programmes across the NHS.

Throughout, the campaign emphasised the simple approach that could be taken to change practice. Providing purposefully simple audit tools, or monitoring tools to focus on one aspect of care such as recording observations to make change easier. This was further emphasised during *Patient Safety First Week* with a strapline of 'one new step' and the subsequent focus weeks with their single aims for those weeks. Focusing on just five interventions with practical 'How to' guides was instrumental in helping demonstrate how changes in safety could be made simply and easily. A campaign should be thought of as a coordinated set of activities designed to motivate people to take action to achieve a common purpose. If a campaign is to 'win the hearts and minds' of frontline staff, it must be designed clearly with this as a central focus. This approach was considered quite empowering. We found a lot of members of staff felt quite empowered because they had the freedom to experiment, rather than being told exactly what to do.

Clinicians were engaged in a number of different ways through:

- Regular, simple targeted communication
- Presentations from champions, local leaders to inspire
- Expert webinars and workshops
- Targeted mini-campaigns to inspire them to take part
- Engaging their professional bodies or networks
- Providing practical tips

While the campaign had its successes, it engaged and motivated nearly 98% of the NHS in England, but it was still an approach that centred on finding the problem and fixing it. We were missing the opportunity to study the good practice and sharing the learning from what we do well.

Incident Reporting

The NPSA set up the National Reporting and Learning System (NRLS) to receive and analyse reports from all settings, including the public, and to recommend changes. For many years, now safety performance in healthcare has been measured in terms of the number of incidents reported. Reporting of incidents was already well-established in the UK with local risk management systems in every hospital as a requirement of the NHS Litigation Authority I mentioned earlier. The NPSA required these reports to also be sent to the national risk management system (the NRLS).

We genuinely thought we would receive a few hundred incidents a year into the national system; however, it started to receive hundreds of thousands reports, and this grew to over a million a year. Sadly, it was a victim of its own success. The huge number of incidents impaired its ability to do any meaningful analysis of all of the data.

One of the strategies in the early days was to send out the message that an increase in reporting demonstrated a good safety culture. This message was shared across the system including the regulatory and commissioning system who then took the message and ran with it. This led to providers being measured on the number of incidents and an increase in number seen as a success. This is a very mixed message to staff, patients and the public. On the one hand it is good to have the information, on the other hand you expect learning to occur and the incidents therefore to decrease. What an increased number of reports could mean is a poor culture of learning. Also, reduced reports of a particular type might simply indicate that people became accustomed to something happening, grew tired of reporting, or stopped noticing the problem in question. Thus, when reports decline, incident data on their own cannot distinguish between a reassuring improvement in safety or a concerning organisational blind spot.

From a technological perspective and a reporting perspective the NRLS was a success. At the NPSA the only way the organisation coped with the amount of data was to set up a team of clinical reviewers to analyse the incidents that were classified as 'serious harm' (permanent harm) or 'death'. In reviewing this subset of incidents, trends and themes could be identified and then used to mine the rest of the database for similar incidents at different grades. The information gained was then used to issue alerts; notices to the NHS to be aware of a particular risk or to change practice. For example, early alerts raised awareness about the dangers of concentrated potassium chloride, or the risks associated with the administration of methotrexate or the risks associated with nasogastric tube insertion.

However, over time one of the downsides of the system was that the incident reporting was used by the regulators to performance manage units or organisations. The incidents were counted and categorised and each individual organisation was rated according to its reporting rate. This was then published in a league table to benchmark organisations against similar organisations. This created some interesting and unexpected behaviours. The philosophy pressured organisations to increase reporting just for the sake of increasing the numbers. Those at the top of the list were deemed good reporters, but were also at the same time worried that they looked like they were more erroneous than others on the list. Those in the middle instead of using the list to ask themselves what they could do to improve reporting were happy to remain in the middle. This was because they were left alone as a result. Those at the bottom of the list were used as examples of organisations who did not take safety seriously. These organisations were the ones that filled their reporting systems with operational issues to make it appear that their reporting was increasing. What we have created is a culture of mediocrity.

Conversely, because hospitals are judged in relation to the number of incidents reported, staff are fearful of reporting. They want to avoid being the person that compromised the organisations performance record. This attitude to incidents is disempowering the very people who can provide the knowledge on how to adapt and protect patients.

The approaches we have taken to date in the field of safety have stayed the same while our knowledge and the world has changed. Over time incident reporting systems have become one of the most widespread safety strategies in healthcare both within individual organisations and across entire healthcare systems. It is very focused on compliance and little expertise is given to the human side of safety. The costs associated with 'over compliance' and the bureaucracy of safety are substantial.

The problem with incident reporting is that they try to catch everything you can think of (Macrae 2016). The 'easy to see' incidents are usually the ones that get reported the most. This is tricky because in trying not to miss key safety information there is very little guidance about what to collect, more an attitude of *if in doubt, report it*. This means there is far too much information. It also means that safety is viewed as an incident driven process. If too many events are being reported, they are unlikely to be reviewed appropriately. This is an insult to those taking time out or personal time in their busy shifts to conscientiously file the reports.

Incident reporting systems also lead people to describe what happened via a 'list' – so rather than explaining the facts the reporter is instantly expected to decide what happened and tick the right box on the pull-down menu. We know there are there to help identify trends and free text is really hard to analyse but in reality, the information being collected becomes worthless if people are simply shoe horning the incident into the nearest category.

There is a need to collect relevant, useful, and meaningful information through incident reporting systems. Think about what you want to collect. Incidents of importance, new or surprising events – events which have the potential for learning. Make sure it is easy and quick to report and does not add to the burden and stress the staff are already under. Incident systems should be used for learning and not punishment or a threat. Local reporting should solve local issues; national reporting should solve national issues.

Many have suggested there is almost no point in reporting certain types of incidents as we already have too much data. For example, falls, they are a common enough problem at every hospital that you should stop doing incident reports. With so many falls happening one would assume that there is a ton of learning that could be used to prevent them from happening as often as they do. However, we tend to simply count them, quantify, and capture the numbers of falls. Incident reporting systems do this a lot. Capture and count large numbers of the same types of incidents, which is great if all we want to do is count but at some point, we should aim to do more than count and to learn. Simply continuing to capture does not seem to help with our learning. What organisations should be doing is being selective about themes and topics and specify the types of incidents to be reported. This is moving reporting systems much more into real-time risk management and improvement systems.

Capturing the easy to report, or the reports submitted by one profession has a knock-on effect to prioritising action and activities that may not be as important to address as other issues that only have a handful of reports to their name. At a national level the numbers and types of incidents reported are then used to shape safety policy, create patient safety alerts, and other national interventions.

When I was a risk manager, I had filing cabinets of incident reports which would have required an army of personnel to comprehensively examined for trends or to produce useful analyses. Sadly, I simply continued to fill the cabinets. The original ambitions have been forgotten and now all people do is collect the problems. I had little time to investigate and address the problems or to share the resulting lessons. My day was filled with desperate attempts to keep up with inputting the reports into the database, and trying to analyse them to see what they were telling me about the state of the organisation. Incident reports were supposed to help us fix things. However, I don't recall them helping me fix things where I worked. I focused on pie charts and trend data of what got reported and the numbers continued to rise year on year with consistently the same types of incidents reported from consistently the same settings and people.

Both at a national and hospital level the teams are not set up to analyse a huge number of incident reports. Decisions have to be made about how large data collections can be analysed, how areas of risk can be identified and shared across an organisation or across the NHS in order to prevent the same thing from happening elsewhere.

There is huge variation in the quality of information captured in incident reporting forms, whether they are electronic or paper based. The information is often sparse, badly worded, and incorrect. The way to analyse incidents effectively is to use 'key word' searches. However even this is impossible. In a review of the NRLS one of the findings was that reporters spell the same things in multiple ways. One of the most astonishing was that clostridium difficile (a type of infection) was spelt 371 different ways in NRLS reports. This makes it very hard when you want to interrogate the data – putting in 371 key words for a search on incidents related to clostridium difficile is somewhat tricky and time consuming. This is also only one example – when free text is used in a reporting system there will always be multiple ways in which a single issue can be described. The review also found that the data fields are rarely fully completed and the free text boxes range from single-word submissions (fall) to over 800-word narratives.

Incident reports are in the main based on one person's side of the story. When an incident occurs, for many reasons including emotion, stress, pressure, distraction, the truth will be hard to find. We all know when telling stories about our own lives that we sometimes miss things out or elaborate a fact to make a point or even truly believe that we saw something which in fact wasn't there. We know in any aspect of life, that there are multiple versions of the truth and facts. That for one person there is their version of the truth, the facts, and the event and for another there is a different version of the same incident. Incident reports begin with one person's partial view of a complex clinical and organisational situation. We know, for example, that when two people look at a painting they will both walk away with different versions of what they saw. This is exactly the same for an incident.

One solution may be not to report an incident at all. Instead, we could interview people about how they normally do their work and then therefore how in certain cases it can deviate from this norm. Asking in-depth questions about how people work, their working conditions, their work situations, and finding out things that get in the way of doing it well as well as the pressures people face day to day will be significantly more insightful than a short incident report.

When an incident occurs, it should still be investigated. However, it should be done so with the aim of understanding work-as-done and that what occasionally goes wrong, usually goes right. Be cautious about using a linear process to create a sequence of events as this could blind the investigators to patterns and team dynamics. How we investigate matters greatly. Incident investigations should be done from perspective of investigating success not failure.

To understand why and how an incident occurred, it is necessary to firstly understand why and how the same work performance adjustments have been successful in many times previously and then why and how the incident happens at this time. This explains why it is important to thoroughly analyse work-as-done having resulted in successful work outcomes in any investigation. The assumption that an incident has root causes that can be fixed is irrational. Human errors are not the root causes of a failed outcome but the symptoms of poor system and task designs.

What could we do differently? Well to start incident reporting should not be used as a way of measuring safety in an organisation. This is because:

■ Incident reporting systems have never captured all the things that go wrong on a day-to-day basis and never will.
■ Incident reporting systems do not reflect what actually goes ok as this is not counted at all. Incidents are a function of a system that is functioning OK most of the time, a few things will not be right, we can have days when little things go wrong but we got through the day safely.

This is the natural variation of a normally functioning system. When something goes wrong it is unlikely to be unique, it is more likely to be something that has gone well time and time again before and that on this one occasion something failed.

■ The data is skewed as people are biased towards reporting particular types of incidents but not others.

■ Incident reporting systems are used to capture problems better suited to other strategies, e.g., they are used as an 'information system to talk to management'; a way of airing grievances about resources or staffing levels

■ Nursing staff in particular use the reporting systems to share their frustration at all sorts of administrative issues that are not particularly safety related. While these may impact on safety, they end up by drowning out the important information, truly hiding the proverbial needle in the haystack.

■ Very few doctors report safety incidents. Instead, incident reporting is largely undertaken by nurses, and incident reporting systems largely fall under their governance units within healthcare organisations.

■ There is a lack of clarity about what to report and a paucity of feedback regarding previously submitted reports together with a lack of solutions or answers that could prevent the incidents from happening again. Putting it simply they are not helping.

Incident Analysis and Investigation

There are a number of tools and techniques that are used in the safety-I approach. These include Heinrich's triangle, the Swiss cheese model, the '5 whys', and root cause analysis.

Heinrich's triangle – which states that likelihood of a fatality rises in line with the number of incidents – has no basis in fact or research. Heinrich thought of accident causation as a chain of events and that the chain could be broken in order to stop an accident from happening. Heinrich studied accidents and considered that in 88% of all cases of accidents the workers were the cause – he called it man failure. He believed that there was a hierarchy of accidents, a large number of minor accidents and a much small number of serious accidents and even less that were fatal. This is called Heinrich's triangle. The triangle has a set of figures that represent this progression. However, he had no actual data to prove this and as has now been asserted, 'made the figures up' (Dekker and Conklin 2022).

Reason's Swiss cheese has even been discredited by Reason himself. We believe that there are warning signs prior to incidents that we need to pay attention to, but they don't really line up and flow through the holes of a system that also simply lines up for them to fall through. It is far more complex than that.

Reason helped us to understand the difference between active failures or errors of the individual and latent failures that were contributory facts built into the system. We identified with the latent failures which were related to decisions made sometime before an error, such as staffing levels, or resource allocation and crucially we understood that in order to prevent individual errors you should fix the systems. He used the 'Swiss cheese model' to try to explain the relationship between latent failures and accidents. The Swiss cheese model is used to explain the role of defences and suggests that sometimes the defences we build to prevent errors from impacting on our care don't work. That the holes (in the cheese) that are constantly there but usually made safe by these defences occasionally open up when the defences fail, which leads to an accident happening.

The problem with the Swiss cheese model is that it will never provide a detailed analysis of why something has happened, it doesn't really explain the nature of the holes in the cheese and their interrelationships and it does not take into account the complexity of relationships and the dynamic nature of the system. Also, it does not explain what the holes are, where they come from, how they arise, how they change over time and how they get lined up to produce an incident. Professor James Reason himself, who, has spoken and written about the fact that it was a great model to raise awareness of the systems approach to safety but should not be relied upon to truly explain why incidents happen. The Swiss cheese model is a great tool for communicating the issues associated with safety. However, like a lot of safety theories, they are great in terms of their theory but difficult to apply in the actual day-to-day world of healthcare.

The Swiss cheese model has been used since it's conception in safety presentations to demonstrate the impact of decisions made upstream leading to incidents at the frontline. However, the latent factors or conditions may never be clearly identified as many latent factors could lead to incidents in the future. Some latent factors may take many years before an incident happens but many variables will have happened along the way. The model has had its doubters because while the decisions made, sometimes years before, can lead to incidents happening today, incidents occurring in complex adaptive systems are a result of a multitude of factors. No one model will apply to all of them.

The '5 whys' technique is one of the most widely taught tools within the root cause analysis (RCA) methodology in healthcare. The origin of 5 whys is found in the Toyota Production System. Toyota's approach is to ask why five times whenever they find a problem. They state that by repeating why five times, the nature of the problem as well as its solution becomes clear. It asserts that asking 'why' five times allows people to find a single root cause that might not have been obvious at the outset.

The problem with the '5 whys' is that it oversimplifies the process of problem exploration.

Many argue that it should not be used at all. Like many safety tools, though, its reputation is not the result of any evidence that it is effective. It is used because it is simple. When using the 5 whys, depending upon where you start, any investigator could come up with five completely different questions and therefore five completely different answers. It forces people down a single pathway picked at random for any given problem and seeks a single root cause and assumes that the fifth 'why' on the causal pathway is the root cause and the place to aim the solution. There is no logic to this conclusion. Incidents rarely if ever have a single root cause. Sometimes you may never even know what the root cause or causes are.

An article in the *BMJ*, 'The Problem with "'5 Whys"' (2016), provides an example that is used to explain the technique.

Problem: The Washington Monument is deteriorating

1. Why? Harsh chemicals are being used to clean the monument.
2. Why? The monument is covered in pigeon droppings.
3. Why? Pigeons are attracted by the large number of spiders at the monument.
4. Why? Spiders are attracted by the large number of midges at the monument.
5. Why? Midges are attracted by the fact that the monument is first to be lit at night.

Solution: Turn on the lights one hour later.

However, according to others, this example found that many of the details were incorrect. The monument was actually the Lincoln Memorial, and it was not being damaged by the use of harsh chemicals. The real problem was water. Pigeons were not an issue at all, and while there were spiders at the memorial, they were not a major problem. Instead, most of the cleaning was done because swarms of midges were dazzled by the lights and flew at high speed into the walls of the memorial, leaving it splattered with bits of the insects and their eggs. The answers are also incomplete in a number of more important ways. For instance, it only addresses one potential source of deterioration: cleaning water. The first 'why' could just as easily have asked about rain or acid rain, rising damp, erosion from windborne particles, or damage from freeze-thaw cycles.

If the goal had been to prevent harm to future monuments, the first 'why' could have focused on the use of marble as a building material and the choice of building site. The solution they chose of changing the timing of the lights caused upset with tourists and because they complained the lights went back to the previous timing.

Therefore, researchers suggest that this demonstrates that the 5 whys is too simplistic a tool for the complexity of the real world. Systems thinking requires both depth *and breadth* of analysis.

Root cause analysis is a technique used to find out why things happened and to identify the root cause of the problem and fix it. Assigning causes to an incident makes us happy because it means we have an explanation, in particular an explanation we can share with those that scrutinise or who are anxious for the answers but, there are many instances when the cause may never be found. However, very few people can accept that in many instances things 'just happen' and when a cause has not been found it calls into doubt the credibility of the investigator or investigation.

In his seminal paper 'How Complex Systems Fail' (Cook 1998), Richard Cook put it this way:

> Catastrophe requires multiple failures—single point failures are not enough. The array of

defences work. System operations are generally successful. Overt catastrophic failure occurs when small, apparently innocuous failures join to create opportunity for a systemic accident. Each of these small failures is necessary to cause catastrophe but only the combination is sufficient to permit failure. Put another way, there are many more failure opportunities than overt system accidents. Most initial failure trajectories are blocked by designed system safety components. Trajectories that reach the operational level are mostly blocked, usually by practitioners.

There is no root cause. The problem with this term isn't just that it's one root or that the word root is misleading. Trying to find causes to explain an incident might limit what you will find and learn. In the last two decades, healthcare has tried to adopt models used in other high-risk industries, especially that of aviation, in order to explain why incidents happen. The method most used in healthcare is that of root cause analysis. However, root cause analysis is built on this idea that incidents can be fully understood. As I mentioned earlier, they can't. What is tricky to get our heads around is the fact that thousands if not millions of investigations have been carried out using root cause analysis over the last 20 years. Yet sadly the approach has not truly helped us understand safety any more than we already knew in 2000.

The approach we should be taking is to separate out different causes and multiple contributing factors. We will then be able to see that the things that led to an incident are either always or transiently present, it is just this time they combined into a perfect storm of normal things that went wrong at the same time.

As humans we like to find neat answers. There is a belief that when something goes wrong there must be 'a' cause and we assume we will find the preceding cause. Everyone likes a cause, even better if it is a single cause, this mean that the investigators may latch on to a superficial cause to the exclusion of more fundamental causes. For example, if they found that people didn't follow a policy or communicate well or didn't perform a task well then, the recommendation is to 'tell people to follow the policy', provide 'communication training' and 'retrain staff' in relation to tasks. The search for information is stopped when an acceptable explanation has been found even though this may be incomplete or incorrect.

Also, the term root cause is almost always used in the context of negative outcomes or failures, and not in situations where an outcome is deemed a success. We don't do an analysis to find the root cause of success. Successful outcomes in complex adaptive systems come from many factors that come together in a positive way.

It takes enormous skill to conduct an investigation well. Investigators need to help people remember what happened, what they did or what others did. They need to carry out the investigation in an unbiased way, e.g., unbiased by the outcome of the incident, by hindsight, and their own confirmative bias which skews their ability to see the truth. They need to try to see beyond these, get beneath the surface of what can be seen and learn from the data that isn't there, and go beyond the lessons that are superficial.

Investigators need to learn and use an accident causality model. The underlying assumption of these models is that there are common patterns in incidents and that they are not simply random events. The problem with these models is that they perpetuate the myth that there is a neat chain of events or failures which directly cause or lead to the next one on the chain.

Most of the time investigations find shallow contributory factors rather than deep root causes and while addressing these contributory factors may help it will not prevent things from going wrong in the future. A report with a list of recommendations, the more the better, whether implementable or not enables people to shut down any further need for more study. So, the search for a root cause is a fallacy, another myth and this search is preventing us from working on what matters and we end up by working on something that is falsely labelled 'the cause'. Also, the changes we put in place, however good or bad they are, erode over time – we are very good at focusing intensely on something for a short while but we all take our eyes off the ball and resort to our original habits and behaviours unless we make fundamental design changes to the system which makes it hard for people to revert to old habits.

Interestingly, the things we assign causes to are things that are going on all of the time and sometimes they go right and sometimes they go wrong. In fact, there are very few things that can be deemed a preventable root cause, and very few things that can be addressed so that things will never happen again in the future. This is because systems are complex and adapt all of the time, outcomes emerge as a result of a complex network of contributory interactions and decisions and not as a result of a single causal factor or two. Incidents are disordered and there is no such thing as find, analyse and fix. It is important to note also that given the adaptive nature of complex systems, the system after an incident is not the same as the system before it, many things will have changed, not only as a result of the outcome but as a result of the passing of time. So, when it comes to incident investigations healthcare is challenging to understand (let alone measure, optimise and improve) because the investigator has to truly understand the variabilities and dynamics of the system and the often vague or shifting performance. There is always going to be a gap between how we think incidents happen and how they actually happen.

In a complex system you cannot assume that because two events occur together or one after the other that there is a correlation or causal relationship between those two events. By claiming one event must have caused the other there is a danger that a wrong conclusion could be made or even another unlooked-for event may be missed. You cannot assume that there is only one explanation for the observation that is being made when in fact there will be undoubtedly many different explanations. In general work evolves over time, and prescribed work proves too inflexible or too fragile to cope with real conditions. Over the longer term, these adaptations may result in a drift from prescribed policy, procedure, standard, or guideline, assuming any such prescription is in place.

Causality gets confused with correlation. For example, the correlation between solutions and causes. If incident reports reduce there is the danger of an assumption that the solutions that were put in place as a result of the incident investigation resulted in increased safety whereas there could and probably is a multiple number of variables that need to be considered. As Hollnagel says, we associate positive and negative attributes depending upon the outcome. If the outcome was bad, then the cause must have been bad. If the outcome was good, then the cause must have been good. This y makes us feel as if there is an order in the system.

When we report incidents or investigate them we have to consider the fact that our biases can skew our thinking, make us see things that are not there or not see things that are and judge things incorrectly. In short, work-as-judged is affected by how we think about outcome and baseline frequency, the quality of our judgement, our understanding of others' mental states, information presentation, individual characteristics, and penalties and rewards. Will never gets rid of our biases, but can reduce them, some training can help, but it is mainly feedback that helps reduce bias.

The following biases need to be considered in every aspect of safety-I and safety-II:

- Outcome bias – to judge a decision based on the eventual outcome instead of the quality of the decision at the time it was made. For example, ten times the dose of vitamin C for an adult is highly unlikely to lead to harm whereas ten times the dose of morphine to a neonate is highly likely to lead to serious harm. These will be dealt with very differently when in fact they are the same type of incident.
- Neglect of probability – to disregard probability when making a decision under uncertainty – there is a need to stand back and consider the likelihood or possibility of the risks associated with the decision coming to fruition.
- Omission bias – to judge harmful actions as worse, or less moral, than equally harmful omissions. For example, if you do something wrong then you are judged more harshly than if you forgot to do something. It is almost as if the wrongful act is seen as purposeful or a choice when both are unlikely to be intentional.
- Naïve realism – to think we are objective. None of us are objective, we all interpret the world differently even based on the same knowledge and experience. You only have to watch a group of landscape painters painting the exact same view to see the difference in interpretation. However, this also relates to our view that we can be impartial. Again, we cannot we all come with our own take on what we see and whether it fits with our own beliefs and attitudes. All of us are subjective.
- Overconfidence effect – to be overconfident in the accuracy of our judgements and performance – the belief that we are better than others because of our experience or knowledge or status.

- Bandwagon effect –to believe things because many others do. Sometimes this is linked to the 'wisdom of the crowd'.
- Confirmation bias – to search for, interpret, focus on, and remember information in a way that confirms our pre-conceptions. For example, if we have made our minds up that in a medication safety incident a calculation error has occurred we will seek only data that confirms this and ignore any other data that might point to a different 'cause'.
- Hindsight bias – to believe that events were predictable at the time that they happened, to belief that they would have acted differently if it had been them. We tend to ignore the fact that we now know far more after the incident than the people who were involved at the time.
- Continued influence effect – to believe previously learned misinformation even after it has been corrected. This is where we stay convinced about information we first heard despite the fact that new information has been found that contradicts this first view.
- Illusory truth effect – to believe that a statement is true if it has been stated multiple times – politicians use this technique all the time – so even if a statement is false, if you say it enough people will believe it, leading to false memories.
- Framing effect – to draw different conclusions from the same information, depending on how that information is communicated or presented or 'framed' positively or negatively in particular. For example, where information or statistics can be used in a variety of different ways and shown in a variety of different ways to influence people's thinking or action.
- Group attribution error – to make assumptions about people based on group membership. This is where we might say 'all surgeons are ...' or 'all managers are ...'.

- Defensive attribution hypothesis – to be biased against people who are different to us when evaluating an event.
- Just world hypothesis – to assume that a person's actions inherently bring morally fair consequences to that person. As in, people get what they deserve.

Global Challenges

While the NPSA was growing, the World Health Organisation set up a patient safety team in 2002 and launched the World Alliance for Patient Safety. This was formally inaugurated in 2004. The goals were to develop standards for patient safety and to focus on Global Patient Safety Challenges such as hand hygiene, patient involvement, developing a patient safety taxonomy, research in patient safety, solutions for patient safety, and reporting and learning to improve patient safety.

One of the Global Patient Safety Challenges was to make surgery safer. Atul Gawande was asked to lead the Safety Surgery Saves Lives initiative and he accepted in 2007. The experts involved in this initiative decided to implement a surgical checklist. The checklist was carefully developed. I recall attending a meeting in Geneva at the WHO headquarters where experts discussed every single word of the proposed checklist and reviewed from every angle and importantly whether it was implementable across the globe given the huge variety of healthcare systems and healthcare resources. The checklist had three distinct stages:

- Before anaesthesia is administered
- Immediately before incision
- Before the patient is taken out of the operating room

Success at implementing these stages depended on full contribution of every member of the team. The aim of the checklist was in part to create a cohesive team for the theatre session, to ensure everyone was informed and everyone could share any concern they may have at any point. It was much more than a tick list. At the start the team would confirm the surgical site and procedure and that the patient has verified his or her identity and has given consent. The patient had to have the surgical site marked, the pulse oximeter placed on, and tall members of the team needed to be aware of the patient's allergies. If there is a risk of blood loss of 500 ml or more, appropriate access and fluids needed to be made available.

Before incision, the entire team would introduce themselves and again confirm the patient's identity, surgical site, and procedure. The surgeon reviews the steps that will be taken, shares the operative duration, and anticipated blood loss. The anaesthetist states any patient concerns plus that prophylactic antibiotic have been administered if indicated. The nursing staff reviews confirmation of equipment availability, and other concerns. The team confirms that all essential imaging results for the correct patient are displayed in the operating room in the correct way.

Finally, in the third stage, before the patient leaves the operating room, the nurse reviews aloud with the team the name of the procedure; that the needle, sponge, and instrument counts are complete; that any specimen is correctly labelled; and whether there are any issues with equipment to be addressed. The team review the key concerns for the recovery and care of the patient.

The use of the checklist was tested in eight hospitals in eight cities (Toronto, Canada; New Delhi, India; Amman, Jordan; Auckland, New Zealand; Manila, Philippines; Ifakara, Tanzania; London, England; and Seattle, WA) chosen to represent a range of economic circumstances and diverse populations. Data was collected from 3733 patients before and 3955 patients after the implementation of the checklist.

The results showed that the rate of any complication at all sites dropped by 36%, from 11.0% at baseline to 7.0% after introduction of the checklist; the total in-hospital mortality dropped 47%, from 1.5% to 0.8%. The overall rates of surgical site infection and unplanned reoperation also declined significantly.

Some subsequent studies, however, showed little or no effect. Over time compliance was eroded and the stages were seen as a hindrance with some people filling out the checklist for all patients at the beginning of the theatre session to safe time. One of the key aspects of the checklist was the introduction of a briefing at the start of the theatre session and a debrief at the end. While the briefing was moderately successful, the debriefing is often forgotten. The barriers that hindered the implementation of the checklist included:

- A lack of buy in from front line staff
- A feeling that people were being told what to do
- Frustration as the checklist didn't seem to work them
- A lack of clarity related to the benefits and conflicting evidence of impact
- A lack of teamwork with different professions arriving at differing times so the stages were hard to achieve
- Staff who preferred the status quo
- An awkwardness when introducing yourself to people who know you
- The responsibility was shifted to the nursing staff to tick the boxes

Another factor that deterred people from implementing the checklist was that it was yet another practice borrowed from aviation. By now clinicians were fed up of being compared to pilots and air traffic controllers.

In May 2019, the World Health Assembly (WHA) adopted a resolution entitled 'Global Action on Patient Safety" to give priority to patient safety as an essential foundational step in building, designing, operating and evaluating the performance of all healthcare systems. The adoption of this resolution was a remarkable milestone in global efforts to improve patient safety and reduce patient harm due to unsafe healthcare. The World Health Organisation (WHO) launched their strategy for the next ten years: A Decade of Patient Safety 2020–2030.

The WHO strategy has seven guiding principles which if I am really honest do not really take us much further forward, they all feel a little like the same guiding principles written in an organisation with a memory over 20 years ago:

1. Engage patients and families as partners in safe care.
2. Achieve results through collaborative working.
3. Analyse data to generate learning.
4. Translate evidence into measurable improvement.
5. Base policies and action on the nature of the care setting.
6. Use both scientific expertise and patient experience to improve safety.
7. Instil safety culture in the design and delivery of healthcare.

All Change

Alongside the National Patient Safety Agency there were a number of other national organisations related to regulation, standards, litigation, improvement, and innovation. However, just ten short years later a number of these organisations were sadly stopped in their tracks as the Agency was abolished in yet another reorganisation of the NHS as set out by the 2012 Health and Social Care Act. Many have stated that the NPSA was abolished for reasons entirely unrelated to its performance or value. As Lucian Leape says in Making Healthcare Safe (2021):

The chaos of an NHS reorganization that its CEO said was so big that 'It could be seen from space' made patient safety an 'also ran' in NHS priorities. Under Donaldson's leadership, the UK was one of the few countries to make a meaningful national commitment to safety and back it up with structural changes and funding. His strong commitment gave safety visibility and stature. This was lost with the abolition of the NPSA and the redesign of the CMO post to no longer have responsibility for quality and patient safety in the NHS.

Even from the earliest days, the NPSA was under intense scrutiny. After just three years it was audited to assess its performance and aspects such as 'Seven Steps to Patient safety', which had only just been disseminated, was 'found to be ineffective'. It takes on average over a decade to get guidance embedded into new practice, yet the audit office thought it would assess this within one year of publication. In fact, the vast majority of what the NPSA had done in its three years of existence was criticised. This criticism stuck and in a way the organisation never quite got over that criticism, with its demise constantly being considered. I am completely biased but I think we were only just finding our feet when the rug was dramatically pulled from under us, the NPSA can be credited for being the driving force for the safety movement in the UK. It increased awareness and knowledge across the NHS and laid the foundations for the future. These foundations are what we now coin as safety-I.

Sign Up to Safety

Two years after the NPSA closed, I was recruited to be the campaign director for a new safety campaign for the NHS in

England, *Sign Up to Safety*. This was launched in June 2014, as a three-year campaign. It was extended for a further two years in 2017. With the experience of 20 years in safety, 2 years of previous campaigning, and the benefit of time to think about what could be done differently in the future, a small group of individuals came together to design Sign Up to Safety, to create something that built on the past but also delivered something unique for the future.

In particular, the design of Sign Up to Safety used lessons from a previous campaign in the UK, Patient Safety First, together with social movement principles to create a locally owned, self-directed approach to improving patient safety. The key lesson that the Sign Up to Safety campaign took from Patient Safety First (and a number of international campaigns in safety) is that bottom-up change is more likely to be successful if locally owned rather than instructions from the top. It was important that the campaign did not tell people what to work on. In the NHS in particular there are a wealth of targets and central commands. What we have found is that organisations are likely to conform or comply with these in the short term but fail to embed changes for the long term. We knew from our learning in Patient Safety First that the top-down approach to safety led to providers feeling intense pressure to comply with a set of priorities even when they did not believe that they were the same set of priorities that were important to them. The required interventions moved organisations away from their own priorities and also inhibited the increase of local knowledge and ownership of safety. So, our initial challenge was to design a campaign that was genuinely not a top-down initiative.

Our main aim was to focus the campaign on supporting staff. By helping them we were convinced it would improve the care and safety for patients. Too little attention had been paid on how staff feel about safety and risk and how they feel when things go wrong. Too little attention had been paid

to the way in which we behave and talk to each other. This
is what we wanted to focus on and we wanted to do so by
creating a movement. A movement of inspired people who
wanted to build a compassionate and kind approach to safety.
It was while we were doing this that we learnt about Erik
Hollnagel's work in safety-I and safety-II and knew this was
something we wanted to use as the theoretical basis for the
campaign.

Lessons from social movement theory have been
particularly important for looking at safety differently; crucially
the challenge of moving from motivation and mobilisation
to one of action and organisation. Social movement theory
supported Sign Up to Safety to create a compelling case for
change with a focus on spreading energy from frontline staff
out. We found that by not telling people what to do we in fact
energised them. We surprised them and some told us they
found this really exhilarating.

We knew that social movements are not created by top-
down directives, they emerge. They often arise as a response
to intolerable conditions or societal behaviours. We wanted
to create the conditions for others to achieve a shared purpose. The shared purpose of helping people work safely.
We wanted to be dynamic, participatory but also organised.
We wanted to facilitate trust, motivation, and commitment.
Our greatest test was in translating the purpose into action
and outcomes. Without this the initial spark would simply
die down and become a distant memory. We were strategic
and motivational in ways to target effort and organise change
activity. The strategy unfolded over time with a rhythm that
slowly built on the foundation, gathered gradual momentum
with a few peaks along the way. We built a solidarity of col-
laborating with others in a common cause and energised the
people around us.

We began with a launch and a foundation period, as we
gained membership, we generated new resources and as

motivation grew, we celebrated peoples' stories. The campaign instilled a philosophy of local ownership: locally owned, self-directed safety improvement by trusting members of the campaign to work on priorities that mattered to them. We told them that they were the people who know their business or their situation better than anyone. They knew where the problems were. Organisations may not have in-depth knowledge of safety tools and techniques but they know where their biggest risks are. Sign Up to Safety would help them by sharing the existing evidence-based interventions that would help to put things right. We would guide along the way. The campaign encouraged listening exercises with their staff and members were invited to focus on a few things well and to create long term plans.

To further build trust and engagement, the campaign created a brand that was synonymous with kindness, caring and compassion. In today's stressful and challenging healthcare environment the last thing people needed was another stick. We have shown that kindness works; thanking people, valuing them and being thoughtful of all around us are vital to creating the right culture for safety and are leadership traits that we both embody and promote. The question we get asked most often is 'How can we turn the NHS and all who work in it into a system that cares about them?' Key to achieving this was being positive, personalised and telling stories. We needed to find a way of giving hope and motivation. Hope is what allows us to deal with problems and is one of the most precious gifts we can give each other and the people we work with. Being hopeful is about being positive, clear, and consistent.

With a small number of finite resources and a tiny team we compensated for resources with resourcefulness. Messages supported by powerful personal narratives of individual learning inspired people to keep going. Stories made a significant contribution to personal and professional growth as they communicated our values through the language of the heart, our emotions.

Social movements also counter feelings of isolation with a feeling of belonging. Sign Up to Safety created a brand for people not only to trust but to belong to something. By promoting our membership numbers people could see that they belonged to something that was both growing and considered meaningful by others. In the first two years, membership grew to over 400 NHS organisations. Our main methodology concentrated on helping people talk to each other, and provided the opportunities for people to listen to one another in a kind and respectful way via our 'kitchen tables' – an initiative whereby people were invited to sit around a table with a drink and something to eat and simply talk to each other about safety – just like sitting at your kitchen table at home.

A good campaign can be thought of as a symphony of multiple movements that adapts to the rhythm of change. Sign Up to Safety evolved and grew as time progressed. We constantly asked what peoples lived experiences were, what was their 'work-as-done'. Over the years the members were provided with numerous online and downloadable resources. Our model had a central hub of organisers which were connected to all of the member organisations through a safety lead. We created a virtual community, bringing people together via stories, newsletters, blogs, and webinars. Building awareness and knowledge across the safety community, guided towards a shared vision and goal.

Around 98% of the NHS in England joined the campaign and we learnt tons. The key lessons were:

- The way we think about patient safety in healthcare needs to change.
- Caring about people working in healthcare is the key to helping people work safely – in fact we believed it

should be the central driver to improving the safety of patient care.

■ Caring for staff wellbeing is vital; how can staff work safely if they have not eaten anything for 12 hours, how can they make safe decisions when they have not had a good night's sleep for weeks, how can they be helped to safely carry out complex tasks when they are frightened to ask for help.

Shortly after the end of Sign Up to Safety, in 2019, a new NHS patient safety strategy was published: *The NHS Patient Safety Strategy: Safer Culture, Safer Systems, Safer patients*. This is nearly two decades after *An Organisation with a Memory*.

The three strategic aims are to support the development of:

■ Improving understanding of safety by drawing intelligence from multiple sources of safety information (Insight)
■ Equipping patients, staff and partners with the skills and opportunities to improve safety throughout the whole system (Involvement)
■ Designing and supporting programmes that deliver effective and sustainable change in the most important areas (Improvement)

The NHS are asked to:

■ Adopt and promote key safety measurement principles and use culture metrics to better understand how safe care is.
■ Use new digital technologies to support learning from what does and does not go well, by replacing the *National Reporting and Learning System* with a new safety learning system.
■ Introduce the *Patient Safety Incident Response Framework* to improve the response to investigation of incidents.

- Implement a new medical examiner system to scrutinise deaths.
- Improve the response to new and emerging risks, supported by the new National Patient Safety Alerts Committee.
- Share insight from litigation to prevent harm.
- Establish principles and expectations for the involvement of patients, families, carers and other lay people in providing safer care.
- Create the first system-wide and consistent patient safety syllabus, training and education framework for the NHS.
- Establish patient safety specialists to lead safety improvement across the system.
- Ensure people are equipped to learn from what goes well as well as to respond appropriately to things going wrong.
- Ensure the whole healthcare system is involved in the safety agenda.
- Deliver the National Patient Safety Improvement Programme, building on the existing focus on preventing avoidable deterioration and adopting and spreading safety interventions.
- Deliver the Maternity and Neonatal Safety Improvement Programme to support reduction in stillbirth, neonatal and maternal death and neonatal asphyxia brain injury by 50% by 2025.
- Develop the Medicines Safety Improvement Programme to increase the safety of those areas of medication use currently considered highest risk.
- Deliver a Mental Health Safety Improvement Programme to tackle priority areas, including restrictive practice and sexual safety.
- Work with partners across the NHS to support safety improvement in priority areas such as the safety of older people, the safety of those with learning disabilities and the continuing threat of antimicrobial resistance.

■ Work to ensure research and innovation support safety improvement.

Within the strategy it sets out the case for safety-II:

> Safety II is not about writing procedural documents, checklists or top-down interventions. Asking for the checklist or policy on what to do retains a Safety I mindset. Safety II needs a different form of insight; understanding the messy details of work, the nuances and subtleties of what it means to get stuff done despite the pressures, the resource limitations and goal conflicts. So what does this mean in practice?
>
> A good place to start is to teach people how to study what is currently being done, using techniques like ethnography and video diaries to truly understand how people continuously adapt to fit the circumstances they are in. Study the system dynamics – for example, the way people adjust or make trade-offs to be able to continue to provide safe and good quality care when equipment or documentation is unavailable.
>
> People need to know that the act of keeping patients safe is about having a constantly enquiring mind; noticing what happens every moment of every day; noticing when things go right; noticing when they could go wrong; and noticing when they do go wrong. They will then appreciate how they constantly adapt their behaviour and practice to work safely.
>
> Conversations are important. Appreciative inquiry and learning from excellence create a more positive culture and provide meaningful positive feedback. Ask people who complete certain tasks every day how they get them done and what gets in the way of

doing their daily work. They could report problems via an incident reporting system without waiting for an incident to happen; this can free up the whole process of learning as it will not be restricted by any reticence to report actual errors and harm. Leaders should have humility and a curiosity to discover how the world looks from others' points of view; and the self-discipline to halt judgement and develop explanations for why people do what they do.

Integrating Safety II, complexity science and implementation science could result in tailored solutions which factor in everyday situations and take account of complexity when translating research into practice. Instead of simplistic solutions to a complex problem, more sophisticated models would work better for the unpredictability and uncertainty of a complex system. And instead of seeing the variables in the system as difficulties to overcome, they would be seen as normal conditions to work with. This also moves from a 'one size fits all' approach to a realist view of healthcare, one that it is made up of multiple different types of sub organisational units.

As part of the strategy implementation, people will be given the skills to take a safety II approach and embed training in learning from what goes well alongside other prospective safety improvement techniques in the new *national patient safety syllabus*. Safety II principles are also being embedded in the reporting system that will replace the NRLS.

Still Not Safe

Over the years there have been a number of publications questioning the approach we have taken in safety. In 2020 a book was published which, for me, summarised that journey beautifully. This was the book *Still Not Safe* by the late Robert L. Wears and Kathleen Sutcliffe. The authors examined the safety movement and tried to understand why it has failed to deliver the gains promised over two decades of research, funding, and policymaking. The authors state that almost 20 years after the start of the safety movement, patients are still experiencing harm from the care they receive and, in many ways, facing the same problems over and over. Still not safe is an attempt to provide deeper insight into an important movement and to make it stronger through critical analysis. It provides a history of the movement and offers a critique of a movement that they themselves say they care deeply about.

The authors assert, as many do, there is an absence of consensus in the field about aspects of safety, little agreement on what preventable harm actually is or what constitutes an error, and the collection of information is subject to many biases including outcome, hindsight, and confirmative bias. The authors describe how the approaches we have taken to date may in fact deepen the problems within the safety movement. There is still a tendency to place blame for incidents on the people on the frontline and this tendency creates an environment where workers are less likely to report incidents when they occur. Moreover, these people are also less likely to report structural problems they encounter within the system, effectively blinding the organisation to its own shortcomings. The fact is, as the authors state, those on the front line intervene in countless ways to prevent harm. While they are probably making errors throughout their work, they are also able to detect and correct them, making the system more resilient. However, the safety movement has not shifted towards understanding this and examining what goes right.

Wears and Sutcliffe describe the current safety movement as simplistic and myopic, borrowing concepts from other industries but applying them superficially and in isolation without a comprehensive, systematic approach. This is similar to the viewpoint of other safety experts who are now disputing the assertions that have been made over the years and the tools that we have all been using.

Wears and Sutcliffe suggest in *Still Not Safe* that the field of safety needs to diversify. As the research field has grown, they argue, it has increased the concentration of medical professionals within its ranks, and that consolidation around medicine edges out safety scientists from other fields such as engineering and psychology who could diversify the thinking and approaches to safety.

There are many of us who consider that progress in safety has been too slow and we welcomed this book. It is an important reflection for us all to consider for the future. In particular, it highlighted the problems with the different concepts we had adopted. Are we any safer than we were in the year 2000? Slowly, almost insidiously, this thought has crept into my work.

Part 2

Where Do
We Want to Be?

What Is Safety-II?

As we have seen in Part 1, over time safety experts have come to believe that there are some foundational core concepts that need to be changed if we are to achieve meaningful improvement in safety. Returning to the statistic of 10% of patients harmed as a result of the care provided to them, one could ask, what about the 90%? What is happening in the 90% of care? If we looked we would find functioning systems, not necessarily perfect, but functioning nonetheless. If we look at safety as care going well then surely this information resides in the 90%, and surely we would want to know more about this.

As Erik Hollnagel would say, *what is happening when nothing bad is happening?*

Most of the time what we do goes ok. However, in our current safety world, we focus on the 10% as a way of understanding whether a system is safe or not, but we are only actually understanding the system when it fails. The failure is only a tiny portion of what is going on. If we instead try

DOI: 10.4324/9781003180296-2

to understand the 10% and 90%, we can put the failure into perspective, we can perhaps truly understand how safe our systems, processes, and practices are. This requires us to study 'work-as-done': how things unfold as they should, as they are expected or planned today together with when the unexpected or unplanned happens.

Safety-II is a way to understand the realities of everyday work in a constructive and positive way. It is a way to become more proactive and preventative, helping reduce the risks and minimise their effects. It explicitly assumes that systems work because people are able to adapt and adjust what they do to match the conditions they face. Currently, the safety-I view does not take into account that human performance practically always goes right and things go right because people adjust what they do to match the conditions of work.

Safety-II is a different interpretation of what it means to be safe. In fact, Erik Hollnagel (2014) would say that the word 'safety' is not actually about safety at all, that it is about ensuring an organisation, department, unit, or team functions as intended. It isn't a new initiative or product for people to implement, but much more about a different way of looking at safety using a different mindset, to move beyond the traditional focus on failure and to consider wider issues of systems and how they function.

Safety-II is also about the way we interact with each other and the way we behave as much as the technical aspects of what we do. It emphasises mutual respect, a non-tolerance of disrespectful behaviours and enables people to feel safe to participate and speak up.

Healthcare staff are able to detect and correct when something goes wrong or when it is about to go wrong and intervene before the situation becomes seriously worsened. The result of all this is performance variability, not in the negative sense where variability is seen as a deviation from some norm or standard, but in the positive sense that variability represents the adjustments that are the basis for safety. However, in our current approach there is an attempt to reduce errors and incidents by standardisation and constraining variability. This is through training, guidelines, policies, procedures, rules, and regulations as well as supervision and standardised processes, forcing healthcare staff to stick to the rules. This interestingly can lead to unproductive or even unsafe care.

Risk Resilience

Safety-II was coined by Erik Hollnagel, a risk resilience engineer. Risk resilience is the capacity to prevent minor mishaps from getting worse or a minor incident becoming a serious one. The methods are focused on how safety can be maintained and an understanding of what is acceptable risk and unacceptable risk. Those working in risk and risk resilience have for some time now understood the need to be far more proactive if we are doing to build safer systems. A resilient system is one that continually revises its approach to work in an effort to prevent or minimise failure. It is about being constantly aware of the potential for failure and helping people make decisions knowing the system is already compromised because it includes sometimes faulty equipment, imperfect processes, and fallible human beings. Hollnagel and his risk resilience colleagues (2015) describe three key elements as part of resilience:

- Foresight or the ability to predict something bad happening
- Coping or the ability to prevent something bad becoming worse
- Recovery or the ability to recover from something bad once it has happened

Resilience offers a proactive and positive system-based approach, allowing people to understand both what sustains and what erodes the ability to adapt to changing pressures. People learn how to stay 'safe', rather than focusing on error as an end in itself. The humans in the system are a primary source of resilience in creating safety. Conklin (2020) outlines four components of risk resilience:

1. Fixate on where the next failure will happen. Don't be surprised by failure. Constantly look for areas that are confusing, risky, or under high pressure. We cannot predict the next incident, but we can predict environments where events and failures are more likely to happen.
2. Constantly strive to reduce complexity. Ask what would make work easier to do.
3. Understand what the processes are serving. Are we trying to improve the operational aspects and governance of the system or the outcome of care? As time goes by rules and policies drift towards maintaining compliance with governance, not about achieving a good outcome.
4. Respond to low-level signals seriously. Go out there, and fix the problem and respond to events purposefully. Don't go out to fix the individual, don't enact immediate policy and rule change. Slow down and learn. The only way that change can ever happen, the only way incidents are prevented, is through learning.

Human Factors

In addition to those that work in risk resilience, there are experts who work in the field of human factors and ergonomics, who are also at the forefront of thinking differently about safety. The aim of human factors is to create high-reliability and resilient healthcare systems. The discipline is concerned with understanding interactions among humans and other elements of a system. It has focused in other industries on design of equipment, environments, communication, handling of emergencies, simulation, teamwork.

One of the biggest contrasts between healthcare and other high-risk industries is the emphasis given by the latter to human factors in understanding how safety problems develop and how this knowledge can be applied to building a system's defences to make it more resilient to things going wrong. Over the last two decades, healthcare leaders and managers have been interested in the benefits to their health systems of the human factors approach and the potential gains in improved performance in safety. However, implementation has so far been on a very limited scale.

Using human factors can help support human performance, effectiveness, system design, and safety in healthcare. The human factors approach takes into account the people in the system, their environment, their surroundings, the physical context, as well as the policies, procedures, teamwork, risks, culture, structure, and regulations. There are multiple factors that impact on performance: mental workload, fatigue, boredom, distractions, device design, and the use of professional language such as acronyms and abbreviations.

There is a theory found in the human factors literature of situational awareness and relates to the measurement of human performance within complex, real-world situations. Situational awareness is defined as a constantly evolving picture of the state of the environment.

- How do individuals use the information once it is observed?
- How do they explain their environment?
- How do they predict what might happen next?

It is through situational awareness that healthcare workers start to recognise the subtle cues that might not quite fit. They actively seek out data from around them to figure out what is going on now and what the impact for the future might be. This is another component of the safety-II approach.

A key component of the field of human factors is systems thinking. Safety-II arises from the use of systems thinking and the tools of a systems thinker. These are to study the whole system: the processes and activities that are disconnected or isolated, the interconnections and relationships, the silos and the things that link up the silos. Systems thinking uses analysis and synthesis to help us understand how systems work. This means understanding what makes them work, what produces poor results, and what produces good results, and, importantly, how to shift them into better behaviour patterns. As healthcare continues to change rapidly and become more complex, systems thinking is vital to help us manage, adapt, and consider the choices we have before us. It is also vital as part of any investigation that is required following an incident.

For too long in safety we have focused on problems in isolation, one harm at a time. Across the UK there are projects and people who focus on falls, pressure ulcers, sepsis, acute kidney injury, or venous thrombus embolism (VTE), the list goes on. These individuals and teams are passionate about their particular area. They 'lobby' people for attention, bring people together to help reduce or eliminate specific harms through a project-by-project approach. What this approach can do is create competing priorities. It can confuse those at the frontline, as they don't know which 'interest' or area of harm deserves more or less effort, time, and resource.

The system approach to safety would steer us away from this silo approach to a more holistic, systematic approach. Working on the factors or variables that are common to or thread throughout all of the individual areas of harm; a common set of causal or contributory factors. These are, for example, communication, patient identification, patient observations, the sharing of information with each other and patients, the deficiencies in teamwork and team culture, and the way we design the system, equipment and tasks, and the care pathway. These cross-cutting factors happen time and time again. In addition to the focus on these cross-cutting or common human factors, healthcare needs to invest in designers and develop procurement policies that support where possible appropriate standardisation of equipment and care processes. The system approach teases out the poor design or imperfect systems which are to blame for patient harm and not the individuals that work in them. It helps us understand the system and design solutions that fit for the different systems at place. It helps us design solutions that change the system not the people.

Complex Adaptive Systems

In order to apply safety-II in healthcare, it is necessary to understand how our systems function, the properties and characteristics of the entire system including the independent and interdependent processes and relationships that make up the system.

Healthcare is a complex adaptive system. A dynamic network of people and tasks acting in parallel, constantly reacting to what the other people and tasks are doing, which in turn influences behaviour, decisions, and choices. Healthcare is extraordinarily complex and has transformed over the last three decades. If we thought it was complex before 2020 then our world has just sent that skyrocketing. If we are going to address this complexity, we need to change our approach to safety.

A complex adaptive system has aspects within it that are simple, complicated, and complex.

A complicated system can be assembled from its parts – follow the handbook and you can build something that is complicated. It requires some skill to assemble but if you follow step by step, you can achieve the end result. Think Ikea flatpack. A complicated system is one where you can usually predict what is going to happen but a complex system is where there are too many interactions and interdependencies to be able to predict with absolute certainty any outcome. In healthcare we are not confronted with problems that are independent of each other. All problems are situated within dynamic systems that are constantly changing and numerous people that interact with each other.

A complex system is where the parts are moving all of the time and there is a dynamic nature to the relationships between each of the parts. Bringing up a child is a complex task. The human body is a complex system. So is healthcare. In healthcare we have a whole bunch of people working in different parts of the system: acute care, mental health, ambulance services, community services, general practice, and so on. Within those areas there are multiple specialists, technicians, clinicians, managers, procurers, designers – I could go on forever – who are all, every single one, a key component of the ecosystem that is healthcare. As you read this, one of them is you.

Too often we try to simplify healthcare and create solutions that are supposed to fit everywhere. We look at complicated or complex problems and seek simple solutions that are inappropriate for the degree of complexity. Interventions that are not designed for complex systems will not make a difference to the everyday reality. Safety-II forces us to consider the dynamic and non-dynamic properties of healthcare and the varying characteristics, forces, variables, and influences across it. If we want to change or improve or strengthen a complex system like healthcare, we need to look for patterns in the behaviour of the system. We need to look for interconnections within the system rather than isolated problems.

Within healthcare there are multiple moving parts. We have realised over time that making changes one problem at a time in isolation was not going to make healthcare safer. In a complex adaptive system, any change made will impact on the other components of the system, in both good and bad ways. There will be unintended consequences which can and will ripple out and out. The crucial concept to grasp is that our current problems are too complex for either individuals to solve on their own or for isolated incidents to be addressed on their own. We need the collective intelligence. Once you start to see these parts as they interact every day you can notice the trends, and those trends as symptoms of underlying system structure, you will be able to consider new ways to manage and new ways to work in a complex adaptive system. Success is dependent upon understanding the intricate web of connections.

Stop. Take out a piece of paper and grab a pen. Write down everything you can see where you work: the people, the reception, nurses' station, offices, computers, desks, operating theatre equipment, infusion pumps, sinks, cupboards, and so on. Once you start listing the elements of your system it feels never-ending. Then think about the interconnections – how are all of these elements connected and how do they interact with each other. Think about how the information and people make their way through the system and how the people are impacted by the resources, conditions, culture, behaviours, and attitudes. Think about the things that are supposed to guide us or things that we are given: the policies and procedures, rules and requirements, staffing and budgets. All of these impact on operational decision-making and how we communicate.

There are different types of people, different professions, levels, roles, skills all working with other different people.

Different schedules, rotas, rules, boundaries, habits, customs, languages. All of these people are interacting constantly, adapting and adjusting as they move around. Every day the work is dynamic, constantly changing with patients requiring care in the exact time other patients require the same care and staff who are required to adapt and be flexible all of the time.

Those that work in healthcare often work in fast-paced environments and unsafe working conditions or processes, with high physical work demands. In such stressful and often hazardous work environments, the safety of patients is the first priority but has also the potential to be the first to be impacted when staff are not able to perform safely. Safety requires constant mental astuteness to oversee the needs of fragile, vulnerable, compromised, ill people in unpredictable settings. The more complex the work is to perform the higher likelihood for error, yet we place frontline staff in more and more complex environments and are shocked when they make more mistakes. Complexity always creates error opportunities and can lead to people adapting and adjusting a rule (violation) in order to maintain safety.

The problem with linear thinking is that healthcare is far from a linear system, and outcomes are emergent rather than resultant. Importantly, we need to be careful when attributing cause and effect in a complex adaptive system. As the system is dynamic, it does not necessarily respond to intended change as predicted. Healthcare delivery is also transitory; so even if there is an attempt to understand it at one time, it will have changed before that understanding has been fully explained.

The current safety models and methods assume that systems are linear with resultant outcomes. The work we did in the early days was grounded in assumptions and generalisations that are now either wrong or lacking context. Linear thinking is one of them. Linear thinking is when we consider that one thing leads to another in a stepwise fashion, like a production line, and the solutions are found in policies, procedural guidelines, rules, regulations. For linear systems, standardisation is the dream.

Traditional approaches to safety apply linear tools and solutions to our complex adaptive system, in an attempt to understand it, to constrain and avoid variability and work-arounds, and to investigate it when things don't go as planned. Hollnagel's view is that simple linear accident models were appropriate for the work environments of the 1920s (when they were first conceived) but not for the current work environments. Today we are not finding out why things happen sometimes to some people and not to others. We are not finding out what difference the relationships and connections make to safety. Thinking in a linear way about complex, multidimensional challenges is one of the biggest obstacles to safety. It prevents people from moving towards a systems approach to change.

We are not a linear system. A general practice surgery or a labour ward or an intensive care or emergency department cannot be taken apart in a meaningful way and the functions are not bimodal, neither in detail nor for the system as a whole. However, until now we have used all sorts of tools and tried our best to learn from industries that are dominated by linear systems – such as car production lines or even aviation. Work that lends itself to a straight-line design.

Traditional linear thinking does not account for complexity. These industries require reliability – as in they need the system to function the same every single time – and are not met with the same number of variables as healthcare. Aviation, for example, is filled with people who use the services of that industry but is in the main less concerned at the differences of those people and sees them as simply human beings who want to travel from one place to another. Complexity models attempt to move us away from the naivety of conventional linear or straight-line thinking and causality, i.e., 'if we do x it will inevitable result in y' or 'z happened because of x followed by y followed'. I will explore this in more detail in the section titled 'Complexity'.

Safety incidents are viewed as the result of a sequence of events. This linear way of hypothesising the order of events was put forth by Heinrich in 1931 and is still commonplace today. This model puts forth that everything preceding an incident occurs in a linear way, in an order. It is also referred to as the domino model, showing an incident as the last in a line of falling dominoes.

What we should be doing is to capture and understand all the things that are happening prior to a failure by both look-ing at the (linear) timeline of the event (which will never be truly representative of reality), and at the same time look at the complex relationships that exist between all the many moving parts that impacted on the outcome.

Within the complex adaptive system there are a variety of different approaches to risk. Vincent and Amalberti (2016) and others have described these are:

■ Ultra-adaptive
■ High-reliability
■ Ultra-safe

Ultra-adaptive systems are where risk is part and parcel of the work. An ultra-adaptive system requires experts who prosper in adverse conditions and can adapt and adjust accordingly. Examples of an ultra-adaptive environment include emer-gency medicine or community general practice (GP). These are areas that have a very high level of autonomy and there is no prior knowledge of the issues that the patients will present before they arrive. Areas like emergency medicine and other ultra-adaptive environments will never be free from risk and the potential for harm. The key is to understand how we can help those who work in an ultra-adaptive system to adapt and respond to the difficult situations they face. Ultra-adaptive systems do not lend themselves to detailed prescription, policies, or protocols. They are dependent upon a culture of trust.

High-reliability systems are where risk is managed and controlled as far as possible, with the acknowledgement that things could and will fail occasionally. Staff in these areas need to be allowed to adapt but are also expected to follow a certain level of rules and procedures; there is a need for some prescribing but also need to be able to adapt when needed. Examples of a high-reliability system are anaesthesiology, surgery, obstetrics, and midwifery. These areas are reliant on personal skill but can be more prepared and disciplined, and the risks while not entirely predictable are known and understood. In these areas the management of risk should be a constant concern.

Karl Weick and Kathleen Sutcliffe (2007) have distilled five characteristics of a high-reliability system:

1. Preoccupation with failure. High-reliability systems treat every small lapse as a potential symptom of an important system weakness that could have major consequences down the track.
2. Reluctance to simplify. People who work in high-reliability systems are unwilling to respond to the complexity of processes, technologies, and delivery environments by adopting a simplified view of them in order to stay focused on a small number of key tasks. Some aspects of understanding a complex operation can be simplified, but a much more nuanced and holistic acceptance of the complex elements and how they are interconnected is essential to staying safe.
3. Sensitivity to operations. There is a strong emphasis on paying attention to how small changes affect the rest of system. It involves a widened perspective so that focusing on one thing does not have negative repercussions on another. Sensitivity to operations is about the work itself,

about seeing what we are actually doing, regardless of intentions, designs, and plans.

4. Commitment to resilience. The hallmark of a high-reliability system is not that it is error-free, but that errors do not disable it, keeping errors small and allowing continued safe functioning.

5. Deference to expertise. High-reliability systems have a policy of cultivating diversity in profession and role so that someone will understand each of the complex aspects of the system. Authority will migrate to the person with the greatest expertise, irrespective of their status. Hierarchies are generally bad for maintaining safe systems, as is deference to authority rather than to expertise.

Ultra-safe systems are where risk is excluded as far as possible. This is a system that lends itself to regulation and supervision to avoid exposing frontline staff and patients to unnecessary risk. Examples of an ultra-safe areas are the administration of blood transfusion, chemotherapy, microbiology, and radiotherapy. These areas are reliant on standardisation, automation, and the avoidance of risk wherever possible. The skills required in these areas are knowledge and execution of standard operating procedures and practised routines. This approach also relies on external oversight, rules and regulation, and an ability to prescribe care in detail. In fact, these areas require as much detail as possible to be written down. For example, the delivery of chemotherapy requires a high degree of accuracy in terms of the amount prescribed and a clear adherence to rules around prescribing and administration.

As explained, healthcare is made up of all three of these systems and yet we try to create a blanket approach to risk, policies, and procedures which is applicable only to ultra-safe systems. Ultra-safe systems would not work or be appropriate for the majority of healthcare. The vast majority of what we do in healthcare cannot be prescribed minute by minute and indeed if we did do so and expected staff to follow these in detail, they would be stifled to the point of an inability to act. As much as we desire completely predictable work, work without surprises and variability, we simply don't live and work in a world where perfection happens in complex systems (Dekker and Conklin 2022).

A patient will experience all of these different approaches during an episode of care. For example, a patient who is in a road traffic accident will be treated by paramedics and the ambulance service who will need to respond in an ultra-adaptive way. The patient will need to be assessed, diagnosed, and treated in accordance with not only what has happened to them but where it has happened. The patient will then be transported to the emergency department who will also need to react to the patient's condition which will change over time. The patient may require surgery and then they get to experience the high-reliability approach of anaesthesiology and surgery together with post-operative recovery and ward care. During their time in hospital, they may be given a blood transfusion and will undoubtedly be tested and, if necessary, treated for infection and electrolyte imbalance which require an ultra-safe approach. The patient may have needed resuscitation and defibrillation which also require an ultra-safe approach to administration in terms of the right amount of medication and delivery of shock treatment.

Part 3

How Do We Get There?

Safety-I and Safety-II

There is a myth that safety-II replaces safety-I and all we need to do is study success and ignore the failure. This is not correct. Safety-II does not replace safety-I. It is both. An appreciation of both the 10% and the 90% will lead to healthcare staff have a better way of understanding and addressing safety. Safety-II was coined by Erik Hollnagel and colleagues and arises from resilience and resilience engineering (2015). Some argue that if safety-I is our current approach, and safety-II is the evolution of that, then surely the combination of the two should be safety-III. Hollnagel has rejected this.

As healthcare becomes more complex, adjustments become increasingly important to maintain a functioning system. The challenge for those that work in safety is to understand these adjustments – in other words, to understand how performance usually goes right in spite of the uncertainties, ambiguities, and goal conflicts that pervade complex work situations. How it works day in day out.

It is important to remember that safety-I methods may be sufficient for certain circumstances and in fact it may be simply the way they have been applied that is the problem, not the

DOI: 10.4324/9781003180296-3   **103**

methods themselves. Healthcare staff learn to identify and over-come the flaws in the system and processes they work with and have the ability to deal with the actual demands and adjust their performance accordingly. They importantly interpret and apply policies and procedures to match the conditions.

Currently there is a need to work out how we can do this effectively, bring the two together, to demonstrate how they inter-act with each other and how they may be implemented together. Simply looking at safety through one or other of these two con-cepts would not achieve the changes we all seek. Bringing the two together draws out attention to factors we would not other-wise consider. It is a collective knowledge. Of course, it is abso-lutely vital that we do not ignore failure. Obviously, we want to prevent people from doing the wrong thing, but we are dealing with human beings here. They (we) will make mistakes. Every conceivable thing we do has the possibility to fail. The problem is that we don't know how or when the systems will fail and we know even less about how they succeed.

We know what the different insights these two concepts can bring. We can continue to capture *when things do go wrong* but when we do, safety experts could seek to answer a vital question, '*why has it failed this time when most of the time it goes ok?*', working out how it almost always goes right despite the obstacles and difficulties. We need to understand how effective the workarounds, adaptations, and adjustments are that actually enable healthcare staff to work safely and then seek to replicate and strengthen these. If we use safety-I methods recognising their limitations, they can still be effec-tively used for promoting system safety in many situations. To understand more, we can use safety-I methods wisely acknowledging their drawbacks; there is no reason not to use them, alongside the use of safety-II methods. Although both safety-I and safety-II methods are useful, a lot of healthcare staff and safety experts still have difficulty in applying them to healthcare safety. There is a need to develop more simplified and practical methods to leverage the values of safety-I and safety-II.

People are starting to move the theory of safety-I and safety-II to practical application. The theory is relatively young and requires the world of safety to rethink a number of assumptions made to date. There is also a lot of pressure to maintain the status quo for many valid and invalid reasons. Therefore, progress is slow but growing day by day.

In countries across the world, safety experts are starting to develop the tools and implementation mechanisms for safety-II. In New Zealand, for example, the safety experts are thinking about safety differently. The patient safety 'Punaha ahuru' commission in New Zealand recognises the healthcare system as a complex system that constantly adapts to change. There is also a strong focus on restorative practice.

Study the Mundane, the Ordinary

When thinking about applying safety-II to everyday activity, we can list things from the theory so far:

- Look at how things normally work and improve those functions instead of simply looking at and preventing failure.
- Seek the collective knowledge of staff about their work-as-done.
- Rarely (if ever) is work-as-done exactly the same as work-as-imagined. This is a key principle to comprehend, adopt, and accept. Recognise the gap is there, seek to understand why it is there, and close the gap by looking into your system.
- Have the mindset that the individual workers are not the problem, they are the solution.
- Try to improve people's actual daily work and safety will be improved as a by-product.

- Find out if your staff are reluctant to offer their opinions or speak up if they see a problem.
- Understand that people will make mistakes.
- Don't wait for an incident to happen.
- Focus on building relationships and trust.
- Alongside those with safety expertise, seek out people who are skilled in social sciences and behavioural science.

What do we want from a normal day? We want it to be uneventful, boring even, and definitely with nothing going wrong. We want things to do smoothly and to be OK. OK, not amazing. What safety-II asks us to do is notice the 'OK', the average, notice the mundane, notice the ordinary. There are things to learn from the ordinary, the average. In fact, if we all strived for ordinary, we may not be quite so hard on ourselves when it isn't amazing, when we are not aiming to be superheroes, when we are aiming to be simply human beings.

Ordinary is when we make connections with each other, talk to teach other, tell people what we are doing, minimise the pain or anxiety, maintain dignity, respect, kindness, empathy, and compassion in the face of adversity. Ordinary is being gentle, smiling, reassuring. All of this is the everyday experience that most patients receive. Not a perfect one, a human one. Asking healthcare workers the following four questions requires a small amount of time and effort, but it will start to provide information about the system and reinforce a safety culture:

- What happened the way you thought it would happen?
- What surprised you?
- What hazards did you identify and what hazards did you miss?
- Where did you have to 'make do', improvise, or adapt?

The best way to find out what people are doing is to talk and listen to the people doing the work. It sounds easier than it is because it is dependent upon trust and the ability for people to share what they do. Therefore, those that work in safety need to build that trust.

Therefore, the first steps to understand how we can study the ordinary is to learn about the difference between work as imagined, work as prescribed, work as planned, and work as it is being done. Bring people together to talk about what they do. Change will happen when people are exposed to this learning. Professor Jessica Mesman's research focuses on mundane practices, what is ignored or not considered relevant. She aims to understand the role of the mundane in order to learn and improve what we do. This is through the concept of exnovation. Her exnovative analysis uses video reflexive ethnography (VRE), mentioned earlier in this book. Video reflexivity or video reflexive ethnography is a method that uses video and ethnographic principles to capture healthcare workers in their normal working environment (Zinck Pedersen and Mesman 2021, Korstjens et al. 2021, and Iedema et al. 2019). It is reflexive because it involves those healthcare workers exploring as a group what was captured on the video footage. Visual methods are gaining in recognition in social and safety sciences through their ability to capture the complexities of healthcare practice at the level of workplace interaction.

As Mesman describes it, it is a collaborative method that turns participants into co-researchers. In the last decade she has used VRE to study patient safety in critical care settings such as intensive care, emergency care, and theatres. In particular she is wanting to understand why things go well despite the complexity of the work.

Video reflexivity can be used for single professions and also interprofessional or multidisciplinary teams as a tool for learning about how the systems, processes, or tasks are done well and how they can be replicated, strengthened, and improved. Video reflexivity can help elucidate context, culture, workarounds, social interactions, behaviours. The potential to make everyday practices visible is a key component of safety-II learning; it can help us study the mundane, the ordinary, and the unseen habits of work-as-done. It provides an opportunity to examine what people do every day.

Success is dependent upon a psychologically safe environment and the ability to ignore the camera. The method requires consent to be observed and for that observation to be discussed in a video-reflexivity session. It requires a simple video tool such as a smartphone. The participants in the session choose a practice they do time and time again and film it. The video doesn't have to be too long or even edited by a technician; it just needs to be enough to provide an opportunity for staff to reflect and discuss their practices. Sometimes it requires a familiarisation with being videoed as some people feel odd being filmed and behave differently from how they normally would. To enhance it even further, while the practice is being filmed there can be an observer who will watch and take notes to add further depth to the subsequent discussions.

Video reflexivity provides participants with the opportunity to reflect on any practice and discuss these as they saw them happening. The videos are played to a group in order to have a facilitated discussion focusing on the particular aspect under scrutiny. Participants discuss the video in any way they want to discuss. The facilitator uses appreciative inquiry and prompt questions, to ensure the discussion stayed on topic and explore some issues in more depth. Attention can be paid to the physical actions, non-verbal interactions, verbal interactions with others, the language used, and so on.

When we study the ordinary aspects of healthcare within the safety-II approach, we are trying to understand how the system functions. How it functions the majority of the time. We want to ask questions such as does anything need improving, does anything need strengthening, or does it simply need to be reproduced or replicated in a reliable way.

Reproducibility is dependent upon agreement that this is the way to do the task or procedure. It is also based on the idea of construct stability, that if we undertake the same procedure the same results will happen time and time again. Obviously, this is not correct for a complex adaptive system.

The use of VRE allows for engagement with staff in order to discuss complexity and the dynamic ways in which people work as well as allowing an insight into a practice 'in the moment' rather than from memory. Using video, the team can look at the minute detail of their work. Viewing the video footage of their everyday workplace activities within the reflexivity sessions provides opportunity for healthcare workers not only to re-experience the complexities of their healthcare workplace but also to view those complexities from a new angle. Researchers have described this as being confronted by the familiar in a way that renders it strange. Enlightening the familiar that had become unnoticed. In all cases, the filming provides the ability to have long discussions about people's everyday lives.

Safety-II emphasises the need to shift to understanding how we are adaptive in our complex healthcare systems. VRE helps healthcare workers to focus on understanding the systems within which they work through the lens of a particular practice. Additionally, doing so in an interprofessional group encourages open discussion about the interplay between professional boundaries and may help to undo traditional interprofessional barriers. By viewing themselves in practice, participants can explore opportunities for replication and improvement of their everyday but often unseen work. VRE could help develop the ability of teams to lead their way out of problems through reflexive discussion.

Dekker and Conklin (2022) provide useful action points for staff who work in safety to support healthcare workers in understanding more about what they do:

■ Learn about everyday work-as-done; engage with workers and gain their trust to understand how stuff actually gets done and discover how safety is created every day by work-as-done.

- Learn about the obstacles and difficulties that get in the way of getting stuff done.
- Support and improve work as done.
- Understand local practices and help workers with how to adapt better and safer.
- Safety interventions won't have any staying power if they don't take work as done seriously.
- Find and try to reduce goal conflicts – ask about and identify places where workers need to do multiple things simultaneously that may conflict.
- Help convince others to reallocate resources to alleviate these conflicts – goal conflicts are at the heart of a drift into failure; without understanding them there is no hope of being taken seriously by workers nor of doing much that helps improve the safety of work.
- Facilitate information flows, coordinate actions, and create mechanisms to get information where it needs to be. Coordinate actions across team boundaries to prevent fragmentation of safety initiatives. Get information to those who can make decisions about resources. You may need to prepare them to receive 'bad' news (i.e., that work-as-imagined is not the same as work-as-done) and that there are other ways to support safe working than telling workers to be compliant.
- Generate future operational scenarios; try to sketch possible future scenarios that might come with operational or technological changes.
- The world is not static. Safety risks change as work changes. Without anybody looking out for them, the organisation may unwittingly embrace risky operational changes or descend into techno-optimism.
- Help leaders and others make difficult judgements.
- The organisation has other priorities than safety, despite what it says, otherwise it wouldn't exist. Economic and production pressures almost always

interact with safety. Finding ways to make these interactions visible can support leaders and others in their
decisions.

■ Facilitate learning; keep the model(s) of risk in an organisation up to date. Find sources of blame, hunt down anything that puts downward pressure on people's openness
and honesty (e.g., including an organisation's 'Zero Harm'
policy or similar).

■ Models of risk tend to go stale over time. What may
cause incidents today can be very different from before
the introduction of a particular technology or operational
change. Without trust and confidence that people
are in this together, there's no basis for learning and
improvement of any of this.

Learning from Excellence

Thank you. Two very simple yet very powerful words.
Many healthcare practitioners, well let's be honest many
people, struggle to provide constructive feedback without
hurting someone's feelings. This is the same for trying to say
something positive. We end up by just saying just 'thanks' or
'thanks that was great'. This loses the meaningful appreciation
that we know is so important. Simply saying thank you, as
lovely as that is, doesn't improve performance or relationships
all that well.

I would argue that safety-II provides the opportunity to
do this, to provide meaning to the expression of gratitude or
appreciation. Noticing someone's everyday actions, recognising
that they impact positively on others and telling them that in a
more direct, explicit way is what we should be striving for. We
are not talking about the 'going beyond' the realms of duty
or providing excellent care; we are talking about the micro
moments of someone's day.

Why should we bother? Because providing value to the everyday work can change the way people connect and notice it. It provides people with a platform on which they can continue because they are not filled with doubt as to whether they are doing the right thing. If you don't get this it can be really confusing, 'Am I any good?' When we have these self-doubts our performance suffers. Appreciating and providing value strengthens the psychological safety among the team. It sets the tone for the team dynamics and culture.

How do we do this? Talk to the person themselves, not the people around them. If you witnessed it, you should be the one to share the observation and not ask someone else to do it. Be specific. Describe in detail what you observed. Describe the impact that the behaviour or action made.

One of the most joyous initiatives to enter the safety world is that of *learning from excellence*. This is an initiative that was started by Adrian and Emma Plunkett in 2014 and in eight short years has grown and grown to be a movement across the NHS and beyond.

This is their philosophy:

> Safety in healthcare has traditionally focused on avoiding harm by learning from error. This approach may miss opportunities to learn from excellent practice. Excellence in healthcare is highly prevalent, but there is no formal system to capture it. We tend to regard excellence as something to gratefully accept, rather than something to study and understand.
> Our preoccupation with avoiding error and harm in healthcare has resulted in the rise of rules and rigidity, which in turn has cultivated a culture of fear and stifled innovation. It is time to redress the balance.
> We believe that studying excellence in healthcare can create new opportunities for learning and improving resilience and staff morale.

They have developed an online library, resources, videos, and tutorials as well as printed materials for anyone to access and set up their own learning from excellence programme. This can be accessed via https://learningfromexcellence.com

Mind Your Language

The problem with the language related to safety is that it can silence, stifle, and confuse. Language in terms of the way we refer to each other can belittle. The Band 2 nurse, the agency nurse, the locum, the managers. If you don't use people's names it dehumanises them in some way. It makes it easier to blame them or dismiss them or ignore them. Language in terms of the words we use can isolate. Jargon, complex terminology, acronyms can confuse people and can lead to mistakes being made when they are not understood or wrongly understood. Using acronyms can make people feel like their first day at school, everyone else feels ahead of you.

How we communicate with each other, particularly in terms of clinical escalation or handover, needs to be accurate and clear. For example, a case I have witnessed went a bit like this:

> Patient is given a drug for pain relief. She has a reaction to the drug. That reaction is quite severe and the patient actually collapses, losing some level of consciousness. They recall later that they could hear people calling them by their name but they could not open their eyes or respond. Emergency care is provided and the patient is monitored until they come round but it takes some time so this is a significant incident to both the staff involved and the patient. However, almost immediately there is a desire to minimise this incident. So the language used is 'the

> patient felt a bit dizzy but is fine now; the person
> had a bit of a reaction to the drug but is fine now'. At
> handover it is barely covered, as it has now been put
> in the minor incident category. The patient the next
> day talks to one of the nurses explaining how she
> felt she had a 'near death experience' and the nurse
> has no idea what she is talking about because from
> handover to handover this incident has been lost.

Why has this happened? As healthcare workers we have a
strong desire to care for our patients and not to harm them;
we also don't want to let anyone know that we might have
inadvertently caused something unexpected. We therefore try
to diminish the event as just a bit of dizziness. The patient was
clearly noted to be allergic to opioids and the reaction to opioids described is similar to this episode. But because it wasn't
an opioid it doesn't get put into the allergic box.

Our language affects the way we view the world and our
words have consequences. Language emerges from the way
in which we interact with each other, and it changes all of
the time. It includes slang, jargon, and dialect divergence,
and there can be different meanings of the same word
depending upon the cultural influence. Language in terms
of patient safety is and always has been negative and person centred. Human error, mistake, lapse, slip. For example,
'honest mistake'. What does this even mean? If there are
honest mistakes, does this mean there are dishonest mistakes
too? What is a dishonest mistake? Dishonest is to 'behave
in an untrustworthy, deceitful, or insincere way, intending
to mislead or cheat'. That doesn't seem to go with the word
'mistake'.

Language is pivotal to shifting the culture of safety.
Consider the language you use and whether it promotes a
safe culture or perpetuates the blame culture – consider the
language that opens people up or shuts them down. What we

have learned is the importance of using the right language to talk about safety. Words like kindness, gratitude, joy, and respect are not words usually associated with safety. However, these beautiful words connect with real emotions of people and are needed to build a safety culture which is usually filled with words like clinical negligence, assurance, governance, incident reporting, patient safety, clinical risk, resilience, high reliability, and quality improvement. Most of the time the language of safety has negative connotations such as human error, legal battles, blunders, violations, mistakes, failure, and never events.

If we wish to change the mindset of how we can make healthcare safer, we need to enrich our language with positive words, such as adjustments, adaptation, working safely, positive deviance, kindness, gratitude, success, and optimisation, and use these in preference to the current negative labels.

The language that we use in safety is subtle but powerful in terms of how it impacts on what and how people feel. If people are encouraged to frame things in a caring and com-passionate way, then they in turn may become more caring and compassionate. If we start by asking positive questions such as 'What are you proud of?', 'What brings joy to your work?' 'What do you get right?', and 'Was everything as safe as you would like it to be?', it depersonalises the situation and enables people to say how they would like things to be which in turn is describing when it isn't. When we ask 'what went wrong', it shifts the way in which we look at safety. If we use even simple words like 'what' rather than 'who', it shifts from the person to the system.

Safety II helps us to talk about what works rather than what goes wrong and in turn it changes the tone and language of the conversation completely. It is morale boosting and brings people together. Using the words 'restorative just culture' means we are much more positive about people's actions and behaviours because people are seen as the solution rather than the problem. This creates a more positive, inclusive, and more effective learning environment for improving safety. Hollnagel challenges us to think about our definitions and language when talking about 'safety', that we should move away from these titles or easily boxed in headings (such as patient safety) to talking more widely about 'working safely' (Hollnagel 2014).

Helping people 'work safely' moves things from being owned by an individual or a team to something everyone should do. It moves it from a workshop or a strategy to about everything we do, every action we take, and every decision we make.

Traditional Term	Proposed Term
Patient Safety: this term puts safety in a box, or a role or a session at workshop. It becomes the responsibility of the 'head of patient safety' and the 'patient safety team'.	Working safely: takes it from one person's responsibility to belonging to everyone.
Human Error: focuses on the human as the lead cause for error.	Performance variability: helps us consider the people and the system together.
Zero harm: an impossibility – sets people up to fail and leads to fear of disclosure.	Natural variation: makes it clear that we can never have a perfectly safe system that people will make mistakes.
Improvement: assumes that something needs improving when it could be working just OK.	Strengthen: shifts us to look to strengthen and optimise what works.
Violations: assumes that everyone who does not follow a policy is 'violating' the policy (in the wrong way).	Adjustments: assumes that people adjust and adapt what they do to do their very best for their patients.

Understanding the Impact of Incivility

The problem with incivility is that performance has been found by research to be affected by teams being exposed to rudeness. Rudeness subconsciously impairs performance without self-awareness, highlighting the need for systematic changes rather than individual adaptations or coping mechanisms. The competitive nature of many work environments fuels aggressive rivalry that can easily tip over into manipulation and bullying.

One of the key barriers to people working safely is the way they behave towards each other. Within healthcare there are hindering behaviours such as passive aggression, ignoring, belittling, rudeness, incivility, and bullying. This could be described as a culture of disrespect. A culture of disrespect includes verbal abuse, dismissive comments, and so on. The targets are often those considered less important or different. For example, it is common for nurses to be verbally abused, it is common for students to be dismissed or humiliated. All of which undermine the feeling of belonging to a team, the ability to question, contribute, and challenge. It leads to a low morale and saps meaning from people's work.

There are always reasons behind these behaviours. For example, incivility can mean that boundaries are maintained, or there is less work to do because people don't want to approach you. It helps people take control, gain a kind of respect, and get quick results. Equally it may be that poor performance by others, stress, and low morale can create these behaviours too.

You can either be the target or a witness. But the targets aren't always who you think. Rather than the targets being weaker members of a team, they can be more skilled and proficient than the bullies – people who might be seen a threat.

Now more than ever do we need to care for our staff and help them work safely. Many staff operate in high-demand, high-risk, and high-stress work settings for long hours. This often leads to people working extra hours, working through breaks, and having to work while extremely fatigued.

Civility Saves Lives is an initiative set up by a group of clinicians in the NHS, most notably Dr Chris Turner. The website which can be accessed via https://www.civilitysaveslives.com provides a wealth of facts and infographics about the impact of incivility, curated links to all aspects of incivility, civility, and kindness, together with academic papers, podcasts, videos, and more, which builds the evidence base for why there is growing evidence of the impact of civility and incivility in healthcare. 'When Rudeness in Teams Turns Deadly' is the outstanding TED Talk by Dr Chris Turner which can be accessed via: https://www.ted.com/talks/chris_turner_when_rudeness_in_teams_turns_deadly?language=en

Thinking about Culture

The literature on culture is wide-ranging. Shared assumptions, beliefs, values, and norms are commonly recognised as main characteristics of any organisational culture. The following general ideas encompass what culture is:

■ Culture develops over time, sometimes over millennia.
■ Culture is deeply rooted; it is not a superficial phenomenon and hence fairly stable over time even when different people move on.
■ Culture is shared and relates primarily not to an individual, but to a group or a community
■ Culture is broad and covers all aspects of external and internal relationships in a group or a community.

Changing the culture is not a three-month project. Culture is made up of multiple components: beliefs, attitudes, norms, customs, faith, ethnicity, status, profession, knowledge, sexuality, gender, and many more. When people say *'all we need to do is change the culture'*, we need to push back on this statement and ask *'what aspect of the culture do you want me to change?'*

Safety culture is the interaction between the system and people, the attitudes, values, and beliefs plus the decisions and behaviours. A safety culture is a set of shared values and norms which exist on two levels: (a) above the surface – the behaviours of people who are aware they are being watched, and (b) beneath the surface – the behaviours of people who are not being watched.

A safety culture does not get built by a set of policies, goals, mission statements, or job descriptions. These are superficial fixes that do not produce a shared set of values or behaviours. Equally, a culture of safety cannot be made by issuing a safety strategy document or placing safety notices on the walls or sending out alerts. There are a few essentials related to a safety culture.

1. Control risk. People are aware of what activities are risky and could lead to harm; they are aware of how this could be controlled by risk analysis and risk mitigation but that incidents still may actually occur.
2. Deal with the unexpected. People anticipate and plan for emergency or unexpected situations. People react to unexpected situations in a safe and efficient way. People stay alert.
3. Build psychological safety. People are comfortable to challenge and voice their opinions.
4. Understand workplace reality [work-as-done]. There is a recognition of the impact of difficult working conditions including pressure, problems with time, increased

workload, and fatigue. That these pressures may lead to errors and workarounds. People may adapt and adjust what they do to resolve conflicts or to cope with the changing demands of the system.

5. Recognition that complex adaptive systems can fail in unpredictable ways. There is an understanding that workplace reality is dynamic and continually changing – therefore, there is a constant level of awareness of the threats to safety.

6. Reduce the gap between work-as-imagined and work-as-done. Strive to identify, monitor, analyse, and act upon all relevant gaps.

7. Trust, respect, and openness permeate teams and relationships at all levels. People's ideas and opinions matter. Information is openly shared within the organisation. People role-model the right behaviours.

8. People know what they are doing. Clarity of role and responsibility is achieved. Leadership and communication skills are developed.

Investigating Differently

Investigations need to be about finding out what happened in terms of as much detail as you can. The immediate desire to find a cause should be put on hold. Equally hold off from making a judgement about the facts found. Consider the biases mentioned earlier and the flaws associated with root cause analysis and the 5 whys.

Move away from root cause analysis towards a systems approach to learning. Finding the root cause of an incident is currently an expectation from both inside and outside of an organisation. Sadly, there is never one root cause that must be removed or fixed.

As Dekker and Conklin state (2022 p 70):

> Bad things that happen in our organizations happen because many small contextual factors have collectively combined in such a complex way that a bad outcome could result in our operations. That last sentence is almost the exact opposite definition of the concept of root cause.

In fact, talking about a root cause is unfair to staff and patients. In many reports there is a statement 'we will seek to learn in order to prevent the same thing from happening again'. Root cause analysis misleads patients and staff and provides a false sense of hope that the problems that caused the incident will be simple to understand and simple to remove and fix.

Moving towards a Restorative Just Culture

When culture is mentioned in relation to safety, what people most often mean is 'how can we move away from the blame culture?' I frequently hear people talk about how there should be a 'no blame' culture for people who commit an honest mistake. When does a mistake stop being honest? How can a mistake be dishonest? The language implies a judgement associated with the natural things we do as human beings.

Sadly, today the major focus remains on the individual. We are still concerned with trying to improve safety by encouraging individuals become smarter, make better decisions and better choices. Those that work in healthcare are well intentioned people trying to do the best they can despite the circumstances they face. Over the last two years in particular, this has been extraordinarily hard and many healthcare workers have struggled to find any enjoyment in their jobs and even worse feeling completely overwhelmed. Healthcare has always been demanding but the last few years have seen that demand rise exponentially. Sadly, there are physical, emotional, and psychological abuses that the workforce suffers and in the midst of all of that when things don't go as planned the focus is on finding out whether the people involved followed the policies. In healthcare, this means 'the way we are supposed to do things round here'.

People don't come to work to do a bad job. This is said a lot of time by those wanting to change this perspective. But it is absolutely true of the vast majority of people who work in healthcare. They work in healthcare because they care deeply for others and want to help in any way they know how. So, when it doesn't go as planned, or as expected, or when things simply go wrong, it is rarely down to individual staff and if it does involve individual staff, it is often because they have been set up to fail in some way.

Healthcare institutions wherever you are in the world are teeming with the most amazingly skilled and kind individuals who change people's lives daily. Highly trained, bright, and self-motivated, they just need a helping hand and some really good systems and processes to keep being so.

Safety is so much more than error or incidents but we do need to address our attitude to error. Think of a time when you went to put the milk in the cupboard and the coffee into the fridge. Why did you do that? Maybe you were distracted, maybe you were thinking of the next thing you were going to do, maybe your brain said I need to put one of these in the cupboard and one of these in the fridge and I will put the first one I have in my hand in the cupboard even though it is the milk.

The response to a blame culture has been often describe as a 'no blame' culture. However, this seems to dismiss any form of accountability and responsibility. Therefore, the attempt to address this is to describe it as a just culture. A just culture recognises the complexity of situations and events and acknowledges that while most safety failures are the result of weak systems, there is a minority of situations where an individual should be held to account. A restorative just culture is one that supports everyone when things go wrong. As Sidney Dekker (2018) has said, a restorative just culture is about asking;

Who was hurt?
What do they need?
Whose obligation is it to meet that need?

Three small questions with such a large and widespread impact, these questions have the power to help develop new levels of understanding. These questions seem simple; however, these are not simple questions. These questions are vital in determining the response strategy and in ensuring the best opportunity of moving from reacting to the bad event towards actual improvement.

The three questions provide the ability to listen and learn important information. In seeking the answers for these questions, you will recognise the wider impact incidents have, a deeper understanding. The actual wording of the questions is not very important, but the intent of these questions is. We are learning how the people are impacted, what people want, and how people can continue their work in light of the incident. You can then determine who is accountable for addressing the issues and then these three questions are valuable to providing the foundation for your response strategy.

'Who was hurt' is clearly the patient and their families and friends. It can also ripple out to their neighbours, the community, the people who may be using the same healthcare facility and have lost confidence in the safety of that facility. 'Who was hurt' is also the staff, both directly and indirectly involved. It too can ripple out across teams, departments, and sometimes across organisations. 'What do they need' is about ensuring that everyone's needs are met in a nuanced and personal way. One person's needs may be very different from another's. The most crucial aspect following this is to ensure that there are one or more people who are obligated to meet those needs, not just in the immediate aftermath but for as long as required.

When Dekker uses the word 'hurt' in a restorative response, he is not talking solely about the injury or injuries (although the actual injured party or parties is included in the use of the word 'hurt', of course). He is talking more about the wider and more philosophical meaning of being hurt. He says, hurt is different from injury in that hurt can be discussed on multiple levels of your organisation, for example, people can be emotionally hurt by an event and people can be psychologically impacted by a catastrophic outcome.

It is not a blame-free system; it is also not a polarisation of people or systems, it is people in systems, people and systems. When care doesn't go as planned, or as expected, or when things simply go wrong – it is rarely down to individual staff and if it does involve individual staff, it is often because of the system they work in. Healthcare institutions wherever you are in the world are teeming with the most amazingly skilled and kind individuals who change people's lives daily. Highly trained, bright, and self-motivated, they just need a helping hand and some really good systems and processes to keep being so.

At its core the just culture community believes that blame is the enemy of safety. No matter how much experience you have, no matter how much you have practised, or no matter how much attention you pay, there will always be the potential to make a mistake. A restorative just culture is where individuals can share information openly and freely about their concerns, and are treated fairly when something goes wrong.

When something goes wrong the aim should be to learn and improve and not blame and punish. The desire to blame is strong. There is the pressure to find a reason, to find the person who is to blame, the person who made the decision, took the action, performed the task, or forgot to do something. There is the pressure from the patient and or their family, the managers and leaders, the regulators, and those with oversight.

Because everyone feels let down and saddened, there is a need for healing, a restorative response. This is the opposite from a retributive response. Blame and punishment are forms of retributive justice. It is often see as an effective solution but punishing the individual does nothing for the system or long-term change. It may show strength and power but it does little to build a psychologically safe organisation or remove the fear and shame that prevents people from speaking up and sharing what they know. Restorative just culture is about helping people come to terms with what has happened. Provide patients with what they need and with answers. For staff it is a way of learning, becoming better, and a chance to recover.

People find it hard to make the choice of a restorative rather than retributive response. There is clearly justification that will be needed when explaining to the patient and or their family. It is also really hard to embed this way of thinking right across an organisation. It takes effort and time to raise awareness, build understanding, gain buy in and engagement leading to acceptance. It can be seen as yet another thing to do, another organisational initiative, words not action or even seem as threatening. There will also by some cynical staff and a lack of trust. The pendulum often swings from blame through to no blame with a just culture in the middle. Is the restorative approach a temporary move that people will embrace until the going gets tough and we resort back to a more retributive approach?

Restorative practices have a far better fit when they are used as part of the shift from safety I to safety II thinking. Safety I is closely aligned with retribution, blame, and punishment. The use of appreciative inquiry will also help to build the restorative approach. This approach has a primary aim of repairing the harm where possible. The process requires acknowledgement of the harm or loss experienced, respect for the feelings of participants and an opportunity to consider, and if possible, meet their needs.

Restorative justice now has a significant role in the criminal justice system in England and Wales. According to the Ministry of Justice's evaluation of its early pilot projects, restorative justice was associated with an estimated 14% reduction in the frequency of reoffending and 85% of victims who participated in face–to-face meetings were satisfied with the experience. Restorative practices have also been used in workplace environments to settle grievances and disputes between staff members. The principles of restorative justice for example have been applied to education, where it is more commonly referred to as restorative practice. Here it is being used with some success to resolve conflict and tackle bullying, helping children understand the way their behaviour affects others and how to deal with conflicts which arise in the playground. It would be worth exploring how restorative approaches used in education and the workplace to resolve conflict and strengthen relationships can be applied within healthcare teams to address rudeness and incivility.

Sadly, most healthcare workers state that the support they receive from their employers when something goes wrong is inadequate. Staff feel guilty, afraid, and alone when mistakes are made in a culture where failure is quite difficult to accept. Debriefing or effective mentoring following serious incidents is rare, and leaders often react punitively. This means that staff may develop their own coping strategies to help them deal with what has happened. These can be positive, such as reflecting on and improving their skills, or more damaging, such as dissociation and increased alcohol consumption that are often associated with burnout. Staff feel unable to communicate openly about what has happened to their colleagues and their patients and families. They feel that they will be scapegoated and blamed and thus are fearful of taking part in any form of investigation. This means that the opportunity for learning is missed and the situation can become adversarial quite quickly leading to increased complaints and claims.

A restorative approach provides an opportunity for those most affected by these events to talk about their experience in a process which is focused on rebuilding trust rather than punishment. The person harmed can find out what happened. Staff can look at what happened in a constructive way so that something positive can come from the experience for everyone.

Our reaction to failure will set the tone for the future. People should move away from traditional retributive safety towards the goal of being able to understand how the event happened and to explain what needs to be done to restore confidence and trust. Seek to understand and explain the event to learn and improve, not to determine fault. Seek to learn.

Learning about a Psychologically Safe Environment

In order for safety-I and safety-II to succeed there is a need for psychological safety. Amy Edmondson bought to the fore the term 'psychological safety' in the mid-1990s, around the time James Reason was publishing his work on human error (1990) and the NHS was increasing its knowledge of clinical risk. She did so while taking part in a research study looking at medication errors in hospitals. Edgar Schein had previously noted that psychological safety was vital for people to overcome anxiety at work, especially when something didn't go as expected or planned.

Edmondson says psychological safety is broadly defined as a climate in which people are comfortable expressing and being themselves (2018). When people have it at work, they feel comfortable sharing concerns and mistakes without fear of embarrassment or retribution. This means they are confident to speak up and won't be humiliated, ignored, or blamed. She goes on to say that when a work environment has reasonably high psychological safety, mistakes are reported quickly so that corrective action can be taken.

Attention grew when in 2016 a five-year study by Google was published (Project Aristotle 2016). This study wanted to identify what the most important team behaviours were and psychological safety was the most important of the five dynamics. The researchers analysed 250 team attributes and found the following the top five. Psychological safety, taking risks without feeling insecure or embarrassed, was overwhelmingly the most important team dynamic for a successful Google team.

1. Psychological safety.
2. Dependability – people can count on each other to get things done.
3. Structure and clarity – team members have clear goals, roles, and plans.
4. Meaning of work – the work is personally meaningful and important for all members of the team.
5. Impact of work – the team believe that the work matters and creates change.

I love this list. All of these are critical for safety.

Psychological safety has taken hold in healthcare over the last few years with an increase in articles, presentations, and research studies. Clinicians and managers alike are seeking to understand how we can create psychological safety within healthcare teams. Teams reporting higher levels of psychological safety were found by Edmondson to be more likely to admit mistakes, less likely to leave, more likely to harness the power of diverse ideas, and ultimately, be more successful. We need to work towards a world where it is easier to talk to each other. Where people are not made to feel weak when asking a question or not knowing something. Edmondson describes an overlap of high psychological safety and high performance as the learning and high-performance zone. Starting each team meeting by sharing a risk taken in the previous week improved psychological safety ratings by 6%.

Psychological safety is something that leaders throughout healthcare need to help create. In her book *The Fearless Organisation*, she talks about the fact that sadly many leaders still believe in the power of fear to motivate their staff, assuming that people who are afraid of the consequences of their actions will work harder. Psychological safety is not about being nice, you can still have discussions and you can still have challenge. Those discussions and challenges need to be respectful and kind.

Building psychological safety, you need:

- Clarity – making sure everyone knows what to do
- A focus on outcomes
- A culture of appreciation
- Clear work boundaries
- To be actively inclusive
- To create a narrative that builds shared understanding and creates the conditions for speaking up

- To offer people the chance to ask questions, expand the discussion and provide alternative options, and to respond

When you measure psychological safety, you are doing more than measure; you are:

- Raising awareness
- Surfacing issues
- Helping role-model psychological safety
- Encouraging good behaviours

Psychological safety is not:

- Simply being nice
- Without challenge
- A guarantee that all your ideas will be applauded
- A licence to whine
- Oversharing

Psychological safety requires and enhances a particular attitude, one where people are willing and able to offer their insights to others, to want to share their perspective and ideas. The willingness to share, to offer knowledge provides huge opportunities in a world of complexity. It enhances the interactions and relationships. Even simple small acts of kindness like a hand to hold or cup of tea when vulnerable can mean so much.

There is nothing weak about kindness and compassion. There is nothing weak about having integrity and respect. Safety-II cannot be delivered without compassion, humanity, and care for staff and patients. Compassion is achieved when staff feel they can achieve what they want to achieve, that they are successful, fulfilled, and motivated. Compassion is achieved when staff feel that they are cared for and valued. This comes from the culture of safety-II.

People who work in healthcare are sometimes labelled as uncaring. In my experience they really care, sometimes too much, but factors grind them down and get in the way. The caring is squeezed out of them.

As a leader:

- You can blame and punish or you can help people learn and improve.
- You can judge or you can seek to learn.
- You can be harsh and unkind or compassionate and kind.

When staff are treated badly, this will impact on their performance and their ability to work safely. Being reported via an incident form or having a complaint made against you has significant impact on the individuals involved. People feel intense feelings of fear, shame, incompetence, inadequacy, or guilt. Providing emotional support to staff during this time, ensuring that they have access to people who can guide them through any informal or formal processes will help deal with the isolation, fear, and shame associated with these events. Having access to support is part of both building a psychologically safe environment and for a restorative just and learning culture. It will also reduce costs due to staff attrition, processes, turnover, suboptimal performance, and improve patient outcomes.

Implementing the Four Stages of Psychological Safety

When all of this feels daunting, Timothy R. Clark (2020) has provided a helpful set of sequential stages of psychological safety:

- Inclusion safety
- Learner safety

- ■ Contributor safety
- ■ Challenger safety

Psychological safety is achieved when human beings feel included, safe to learn, safe to contribute, and safe to challenge. It is where safety becomes intricately linked to equality, inclusivity, and diversity. To date the issues of inclusivity, diversity, and equality are in the main considered separately from safety.

The first step, inclusion safety, helps members of the team to connect and belong. Everyone wants to be accepted and have a sense of shared purpose. If we include everyone then we hear from everyone. Sadly, at the moment, those that are different are often treated differently; whether that be because of gender, ethnicity, colour, ability, or sexuality. They are more likely to be investigated and suspended and more likely to feel silenced.

Safety is built upon the collective diversity of everyone across the healthcare team. We need diversity in personality, backgrounds, beliefs, experiences, and attitudes. Safety is gained from the insights of individuals who feel they belong and are included. The wisdom of the crowd works only when the crowd is diverse and each individual feels safe to voice their thoughts and ideas. The safety of any team depends on harnessing differences in pursuit of a shared purpose. Instead, we surround ourselves with like-minded people. This means we miss out on the contribution of outsiders. Therefore, if we seek to build a culture of safety, we need to build a culture of diversity. A culture that encourages ideas from everyone builds strong networks that bring people together to do so.

Hierarchies between and within groups act as potential barriers to effective teamwork and communication. The team leader can reduce these by using briefings to promote a positive team concept, i.e., we are all working together towards a common goal. The team leader can also promote speaking up by inviting questioning or cross-checking e.g., 'if you see anything that doesn't seem right then please let me know'. Valuing speaking up – if a team member has had a negative response from someone previously, then they are less likely to speak up, even if there is a safety issue. Acknowledging and valuing suggestions, even if they are not acted upon, means that team members are more likely to speak up in future.

While diversity is vital, it is worthless without inclusivity. People want to belong. To be part of the gang. Whether it is gender, the colour of our skin, our ethnicity, sexuality, or status. The things that make us different can silence us. If we are different, we have to work harder, work smarter. Exceed every expectation. But also, be invisible, unnoticeable. Don't ask too many questions. Don't contribute, don't challenge. Don't get in the way. Don't be part of the main story, be a sub-plot. Go unnoticed. Become the atmosphere.

This must occur in parallel with creating an organisational culture which makes people feel that they belong, that they will be treated fairly and consistently, and that they feel able to speak up without fear of repercussion. This positive approach will ripple out, ensuring that people feel motivated and cared for. Over the past decade or so, there has been a growing recognition of the need to understand how dependent upon each other are the concepts of safety and staff safety. Inequalities still remain in how staff are treated when things go wrong; staff often work in fear. And some new problems have arisen. As a result of the pandemic, staff feel inadequate, overwhelmed, or even suicidal.

The second step, learner safety, builds on inclusion safety and helps us learn and grow. It allows us to feel safe to ask questions, give and receive feedback. Who hasn't hesitated to raise their hand to ask a question in a meeting or at handover or in a huddle? Those around us need to help provide us with the opportunity and permission to ask questions.

The third step is contributor safety where we feel safe to contribute as a full member of the healthcare team, using our skills and abilities to participate in all activities. This helps our desire to make a contribution, to make a difference. This requires us to encourage others to contribute their ideas. The final and hardest step is challenger safety. This is achieved when people are supported to speak out and have the confidence to ask questions about why things are done in a particular way or to even stop someone from doing something that they think might be unsafe. All of which is crucial for effective clinical escalation and healthcare communication.

Improving How We Talk to Each Other

At the very heart of what we do in healthcare and at the very heart of safety is being able to talk to each other. Talking to each other underpins and is vital for a safety culture. Talking to each other means a conversation. Something we feel is done really poorly when times are pressured and people are stressed. When conversations go wrong it can lead to so many poor outcomes. At the very worst it can mean a patient may die as a result. A good conversation should allow people the time to speak, listening with intent and asking clarifying questions, and observing what is being said and what is not. Talking to each other requires a set of values and behaviours: being kind, caring, thoughtful, honest, respectful, authentic, being human, telling the truth, creating trust, being fair, showing love and appreciation. Talking to each other can also be disruptive, confronting, challenging, moving people from one view to another, moving from the same thing every day to something new.

A good conversation is where the person is given the time to speak, someone listens, and importantly hears so that they can respond. Asking the right and listening empowers the other person in the conversation and draws them in. If we combine conversations that really matter with the desire of the frontline to improve the future we have a powerful force for change from the ground up. We have the potential for something great. If help people talk to each other, one good conversation that matters could shift the direction of change forever.

Everyone and anyone, staff, patients, families, who work in or receive healthcare, we all need to talk to each other. What we mean by that is to hold meaningful conversations: allowing people the time to speak, really listening to someone with intent and asking clarifying questions where needed, and noticing what is being said and what isn't. People know their own situations better than others, they know the challenges and opportunities they face; they just need help to have that conversation.

In safety we want people to talk to each other about the implementation gap, or when they think something is unsafe or when something has gone wrong. There are many examples that show how badly things can go wrong if we don't talk to each other more effectively and what happens when we are not listened to, or we fail to listen or we fail to learn. In the stories thread throughout this book, there are key moments that could have changed those stories forever. If Bob Ebeling had been listened to, he may have been able to prevent the death of seven astronauts.

What we do need to realise though is that poor communication and indeed poor behaviours are often the consequence of difficulties within the healthcare system. Staff are overworked, understaffed, stressed, and yet expected to stay calm and controlled. Rudeness and poor communication will be a direct result of the way in which people are expected to work.

Ten ways to improve communication:
[adapted from Ted Talk by Celeste Headlee]

1. Be present, be in the moment, try to not be distracted by what's just happened and what is about to happen – 'don't be half in a conversation'.
2. Don't preach – don't grandstand – express your opinion but don't be opinionated.
3. Use open-ended questions – closed questions end in a yes or no.
4. Listen, really listen.
5. If you don't know, say you don't know.
6. It is not all about you – don't move straight on to your experience.
7. Try not to repeat yourself; it switches people off.
8. Get to the point – sometimes you don't need all the dates, the names, the details when you need to get some vital information across.
9. Be brief.
10. Keep listening – 'if your mouth is open you are not listening or learning'.

In order to have a different conversation about safety and implement the mindset of safety-II, we need methods for bringing people together to understand how systems are functioning, what peoples' 'real' rather than 'ideal' is. We need to help people talk more about their daily lives. The following are a few methods that have been tried and tested in healthcare for improving communication and conversations and can also be really useful for safety-II conversations.

Schwartz Rounds

Kenneth B. Schwartz was the founder of what are now called Schwartz Rounds. He wrote about his healthcare experience:

In my new role as a patient, I have learned that medicine is not merely about performing tests or surgeries or administering drugs. These functions, important as they are, are just the beginning. For as skilled and knowledgeable as my caregivers are, what matters most is that they have empathized with me in a way that gives me hope and makes me feel like a human being, not just an illness. Again and again, I have been touched by the smallest kind gestures ... a squeeze of my hand, a gentle touch, a reassuring word. In some ways, these quiet acts of humanity have given more healing than the high-dose radiation and chemotherapy that hold the hope of a cure.

Schwartz died in 1995, less than a year after his diagnosis. But his message was powerful, and it resonated with people. That powerful message became Schwartz Rounds which are conducted in hospitals all across the world. Schwartz Rounds are a time where healthcare workers come together to discuss the social and emotional issues they face in caring for patients and families and to share their experiences and feelings on topics drawn from actual patient cases. Schwartz Rounds have been shown to improve healthcare providers' ability to give patients the compassionate care that they need.

A World Café is a way in which people can engage in conversations about their everyday lives and work. The wisdom lies with the people themselves. In relation to safety the safety experts can be used as the hosts. The conversations held are a core method to enhance and strengthen everyday performance.

Huddles can be proactive, preventing safety issues and staff concerns. In this case, a huddle gathers the team together to talk about the day, the shift, or the next few hours. This is different from the beginning-of-the-day briefing because it can happen at any point of the day. Different types of huddles include:

- Formalised huddles; planned huddles at specific times with attendance being mandatory in a designated area and with the huddle facilitated by the most senior person.
- Information capturing huddles; using tools such as a 'huddle sheet' which can list the areas of discussion such as a list of patients with indwelling catheters, a list of patients at risk of falling. and so on.
- Unplanned impromptu huddles; called at any time to regroup, or seek collective advice and can be called by anyone from the team. This could even happen in a patient's room – for example, if they have fallen, it is a way of assessing the environment in real time with everyone inputting their views on what could have been done differently.

Briefings and debriefings, short gatherings, usually at the beginning of a day, a shift, a clinic, or session; basically, any duration of event or time that involves working as a team. It can take as little as 30 seconds to conduct a briefing and should be no longer than 15 minutes. A briefing is best complimented by a debriefing at the end. They both work well if people understand that individuals will behave differently but these different roles or behaviours should be valued, respected, and are all equally important. There needs to be a process of linking and therefore learning from one to the other. Issues highlighted in the morning briefing, for example, can be then discussed at the huddle and then through to the debriefing. Checking in and taking the pulse of the department at any given time. They need to be helpful and focused and create a shared understanding of what is needed and when.

Trio-conversations are where individuals work in threes. Working in groups of three provides the structure. Each of the three individuals have a different role; one person starts by sharing their story, one is an active listener who will ask clarifying questions of the storyteller, and the third is an observer who will carefully observe what is being said and what is not being said. The speaker shares their own experience. The active listener asked clarifying and open questions to help the speaker to develop the conversation, to help them go further. It was not about giving advice or saying what should have been done – it was simply to encourage the speaker to say more. Some prompts were used:

- What did you notice?
- Does that happen normally?
- What might get in the way of doing that normally?
- Do you adapt and adjust all the time to achieve success?

The observer listens in silence, as if behind a one-way mirror. As they listen, they are asked to pay attention to their thoughts and feelings and to summarise what is being heard.

The process is simple yet could lead to unexpected results. Using conversations supports a core human need of being able to share our stories and to be heard – it is amazing what can happen when you provide a simple but profound format for people to really talk together as equals. If you ask people in a supportive setting to tell their story they will. People can be incredibly generous, imaginative, and open hearted. If you get some willing, able, and thoughtful people into a good place to work, then it is possible for them to develop a useful theory about what may work better in their local context. They can also learn quickly. Trios are a way of exploring safety issues without repercussions, where people can understand their daily habits.

Fishbowls can be used to bring people together. Initially start with a large circle for all attendees. Chairs are arranged in an inner circle; the remaining chairs are left in a circle outside the inner circle. People are invited to fill the inner circle while the rest of the group sit on the chairs in the outer circle; one chair is left empty. This method requires a highly skilled facilitator who can help the participants engage with each other safely. The audience in the outer circle listen in on the discussion without interrupting the conversation. However, during the conversation anyone could, at any time, step forward and occupy the empty chair, thereby joining the conversation in the inner circle. When one person moves an existing member of the inner circle voluntarily leaves and frees a chair. The discussion then continues with people entering and leaving the inner circle. The second phase of the conversation occurs after around 30 minutes when the inner circle turns to face the outer circle and the facilitator leads a discussion between the two circles. After around 20 minutes of this, the inner circle then turn back to talk to each other about what they had heard in the discussion.

Simply asking the questions is only one aspect; it is also important to ask them in a respectful, caring, and kind way. What we ask and the way in which we ask, together with the way in which we respond to it, are ultimately the basis of building trusting relationships. Through having a good conversation, individuals can start to build trust, can learn together, and get even better at communication with each other and their patients. Respect is also found in acknowledgement. Acknowledgement is in our words and in our actions, including body language.

We recognise that people and relationships are at the heart of safety and that a structured and facilitated conversation could draw them together, help them listen, and hold a profoundly different conversation about what we can all do differently. Facilitation of experiential learning and reflection is challenging, but a skilled facilitator, asking the right questions and guiding reflective conversation before, during, and after an experience, can help open a gateway to powerful new thinking. While it is the learner's experience that is most important to the learning process, it is also important not to forget the wealth of experience a good facilitator also brings to the situation. A key aspect of our learning is as much about the process, the method, and the skills needed to facilitate as the learning of the actual conversations themselves.

Essentially, all of these methods are ways in which we can help people tell their stories, help people listen, and help people ask really helpful questions without judging. These methods help with different learning styles and different personalities. So helping the introvert be reflective, helping the extravert share their feelings, and so on.

The aim should be to ensure people feel valued, respected, cared for, in a mindset whereby they will feel able to talk and able to listen and able to observe what is being said and what is not being said. Important factors for this include a warm welcome and introduction, an expert facilitator, introductions that don't create superiority or hierarchy, processes that create energy, insight, and ideas. People need the time to arrive, to slow down, to enter a more reflective frame of mind, and importantly, to feel and to be valued.

The variety of methods described here are simply different methods to help people talk to each other. The method chosen will depend upon the size of the group, the size of the room, and the question or questions you want to answer. Everyone's contribution should be encouraged. This isn't just about sharing a story and receiving support; this is about careful and skilled facilitation.

Just a note in relation to silence. Silence is often described as dangerous for safety. It could be a demonstration of a low psychological safety but silence is not always bad. We all have our own way of communicating, how and when we choose to speak up, contribute, and challenge. Some of us prefer to offer our opinions straight away, some of us prefer to put our thoughts together first, take our time, and think about what we are going to say and how. Some people talk over or interrupt others, some put their hands up and wait. Our backgrounds, personalities, level of expertise, gender, age, ethnicity, and language all impact on our inclination and ability to speak up and contribute.

There are some who find silence uncomfortable and will say anything to fill the void. A few seconds can feel like a lifetime. Speaking less in meetings doesn't mean you don't contribute. If you struggle to cope with silence some suggest counting for six seconds. Think about what you are going to say, how you are going to say it, and how you will deliver it. Use the pause to do all of that. The pause that you created in that six seconds can be useful for yourself and for others. It can provide others with the opportunity and space to speak up. Moving on from the six seconds, you could also try the 'one minute silence technique'. After a question has been raised, tell everyone they have a full one minute of silence to think about the question. This stops the most eager and confident people speaking first, while the more thoughtful people are putting together their ideas and response. After the minute is up, ask for contributions in a controlled manner, e.g., by raising a hand. Offer the chance to speak first to those who tend to speak less.

Silence is not always bad but there are aspects of silence that we need to worry about. Silence because people are fearful and worried about what people will think, silence when people struggle to ask the question they really wanted to ask, silence because people have been humiliated when they have spoken – all of these are clearly not great for safety. People who feel silenced are practised at saying nothing. They listen.

Drawing Lessons from Change Management

Change management is the complex process of turning policy or theory or interventions into practice. It is the multiple steps required to take a good idea and turn it into action. If the good idea is picked up or adopted by individuals and then used on a day-to-day basis, it is said to be embedded. If the good idea is then shared across other individuals, it is described as spread. If the good idea sticks and people continue to be different as a result, it is said to be sustained.

Change management draws mainly from the disciplines of evidence-based medicine and implementation science, together with the diffusion of innovations, organisational development, and behavioural change theories. It is easy to have a change idea or design a device or write a guideline that should work if implemented. The hard part is to take the idea, device, or guidance and make it work well every time.

Components of change management are raising awareness, gaining understanding, building engagement, and then the process of dissemination, adoption, embedding, spread, and sustainability. It takes a long time, sometimes years, to turn original research findings into practice and there is a significant sustainability failure rate of organisational change. Therefore, we need to take our time to get it right and provide expertise and effort to achieve success.

Change management requires thoughtful action, and there is no easy way of doing it. At every stage of the process people can and do get it wrong. It needs dedicated resources, funding, and time and a shift away from the short-term approach to a long-term view of change. It is unreal to think that an idea can be implemented through to sustained change in a short few months. This is in part because change requires a culture shift; a culture whereby the embedded idea it still used even when people move on. Making small incremental changes can make things easier, better, more effective, and safer. The challenge is to convince people to change on a daily basis especially if they don't see a significant and large change. Visible outcomes are always great motivators whether you want to lose weight or reduce the number of falls or pressure ulcers. Seeing the graph go down or the weight go off are a great way to convince people to continue.

Change management, implementation science, and safety-II have one key thing in common. Those designing the interventions or guidance that they want to implement must be aware of the impact that they are making. They must seek to understand work-as-done and get beneath the surface of what is going on every day. Help people to notice the things they need. Instead of prescribing steps, people should be able to adapt and own the intervention or solution, fit the intervention within their team, unit, or system. Local contexts differ and as a result people need to vary their actions from place to place.

The list of factors which affect the success of change management includes:

■ Make it as easy and as intuitive as possible.
■ Demonstrate visibly with numbers, feelings, experiences that the change is better than status quo.
■ Deliver the message in person; using role models or opinion leaders to convince others of the need to change; people will implement changes that are liked by other people who do a similar job and the people they respect.
■ Factor in the fact that people don't have time.

- Ensure the quality of the guidance associated with the idea or solution; do not produce a 100-page manual or rely on hours and hours of training.
- Target the audience in design and help them own the change and choose things that they want to change because it improves their everyday and the activity of others.
- Understand the receptive context; appreciate complexity of a problem or the context in which it is required.
- Test it, adapt it, test it, adapt it, and test it again to get everything to feel it fits – shift from the notion that something that works in another country, another organisation, or even another team will automatically work for everyone.
- Reward and recognise people for their actions; thank and value them for their contribution.
- Invest resources dedicated to implementation including protected time for staff.
- Leaders need to use a coaching style of leadership; if they simply try to solve the problems themselves then people will not own the outcome.

Diffusion of innovations is the theory by Everett Rogers (2003) on how, why, and at what rate new ideas are spread. Rogers proposes that there are five categories of adopters as shown in the following image and table.

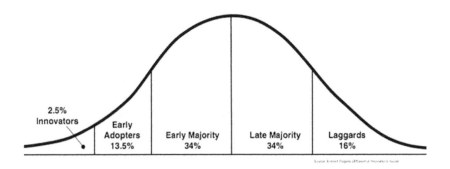

Category and % of population	Description
Innovators 2.5%	Innovators are willing to take risks. They are at the forefront of designing new interventions and enjoy change. They are happy to adopt changes that may ultimately fail but are interested to give them a go anyway.
Early adopters 13.5%	These are the most important individuals in any change process. They have the highest degree of opinion leadership among all the adopter categories. Early adopters are more discreet in adoption choices than innovators. They consider the choice of adoption before they go ahead and tend to want to adopt changes that are most likely to succeed. This category has the most followers.
Early majority 34%	They adopt an innovation after a varying degree of time that is significantly longer than the innovators and early adopters. Early Majority wait to see how successful something is and they watch what the innovators and early adopters do first.
Late majority 34%	They are late to change. They adopt an innovation after the average participant. These individuals approach an innovation with a high degree of scepticism and after the majority of society has adopted the innovation.
Laggards 16%	They are the last to adopt an innovation and sometimes may never adopt a change. Unlike some of the previous categories, individuals in this category show little to no opinion leadership. These individuals typically have an aversion to change. Laggards typically tend to be focused on tradition and the way they have always done things. Research suggests that they will only change if something is made mandatory so they have no choice. Research also suggests that little or no attention should be paid to laggards as the amount of effort to convince them outweighs the benefits of having them on board.

Implementation is a much more complex thing than people think it is. There is an expectation that it is far quicker to achieve than it actually is. Embedding and sustaining change takes a very long time. To reduce this time, implementation practice needs to inform implementation research – i.e., we need to understand work in practice (work-as-done) as it applies to implementation rather than what the research says (work-as-imagined) by the researchers.

Although what is interesting is that as a result of the pandemic the speed of implementation to impact has increased. What we need to now know is whether these are sustained. We also need to know what were the factors that helped this. How did the changes happen so fast? Some of the conditions were lifted, money was made available, but there was also a shared sense of humanity, a shared purpose.

Relationships are the foundation of implementation. Those responsible for implementation need to demonstrate value, credibility, and common purpose. They need to build trust, demonstrate vulnerability, and enter the workplace with empathy and humility. Because changing behaviour is at the heart of implementation, relationships and team dynamics are more important than the strategy or the method. Psychological safety is vital for healthy relationships; it helps see other people's point of view, listen to them, hear them, and respond to them.

Caring for the People That Care

Our emotional health has been impacted significantly over the past two years. Isolation for some, fear for many, loss of social connections, financial uncertainty, bereavement, grief, burnout, and anxiety. Even before the pandemic, for many frontline clinicians the working conditions have been intolerable; fewer breaks, less time outside, covered in protection equipment, fatigue, undertaking roles they have never done before. All of this has impacted on safety and in the way people behave towards each other.

In general, research studies have shown that burnout, depression, and suicide are increasing among healthcare practitioners, and the pandemic has substantially increased all of these problems. The effects of psychological, emotional, and physical harm to the workforce surface in the form of lost work hours, employee turnover, reduced morale and satisfaction, and an inability to attract newcomers to caring professions. To create a safe and supportive work environment, leaders must put in place processes and support that ensure that staff are less likely to experience burnout and are able to deliver effective safer care.

Over the last two years, healthcare workers have been viewed as heroes, in fact not just heroes but superheroes. But as many say, this comes with all sorts of problems. We need to stop calling staff heroes. Many healthcare staff have been placed in situations that were physically and emotionally really challenging yet they had to watch the tragedy unfold unable to react in real time. The reactions were left for the breaks, the toilet cubicles, the journey home, the dark nights. Many distanced themselves from their loved ones in order to protect them so sat along with their fears and their grief. We know the pandemic has led to staff developing burnout. Emotional exhaustion can lead to apathy and having nothing left to emotionally support patients and families. Depersonalisation can lead to seeing patients as numbers or diseases rather than human beings. Reduced personal accomplishment manifests in not valuing patient care or professional achievements.

For many staff they are unable to even take breaks during the day. This means they don't rest, and even eat and drink. They are hungry and dehydrated. Not only don't they have the time but staff report that they are made to feel bad if they take breaks when it is busy and are prevented from eating and drinking in patient areas. They can't think straight. There are also frequent transitions between day and night shifts and many shifts where staff are asked to stay later, or have to stay later because of certain circumstances or even are called in from home to cover when it is busy. Access to appropriate rest areas has been lost. Napping during the night shift is not tolerated. Getting food at night can be impossible.

All of the stress, hunger, feelings of guilt can really only lead to one thing. Poor relationships. People are short with each other; they don't go the extra mile because the extra mile is one mile too far. There should be no surprise that people are rude and uncivil. Because this is not the behaviour of the hero, the staff are castigated for behaving badly. We need to recognise that large swathes of the healthcare workforce will be suffering from anxiety, distress, depression, or post-traumatic stress disorder. We need to make sure that they all get access to the emotional support they require.

Those that work in health put enough pressure on themselves to be the best they can despite their exhaustion without being named heroes. They set themselves unrealistic standards and seek support and validation from their colleagues. The slightest criticism can feel like a blow to the stomach. However, a workforce that is not functioning will lead to things going wrong. Daily life in healthcare can destabilise even the most experienced and knowledgeable teams, thus creating a higher probability of errors and incidents. Yet staff are expected to perform flawlessly at all times, even without effective systems, processes, buildings, or equipment. For more than 20 years, other high-risk industries have recognised that there is a connection between a safe workforce and excellent care. These sectors have pursued systems and processes to ensure employee safety and well-being.

Learning from COVID-19

Sometimes a crisis comes along that is so new that it challenges everyone. It is impossible to write about any aspect of healthcare, or safety (or indeed, life), in the last two years without considering the impact of the COVID-19 pandemic. The global crisis triggered by the coronavirus pandemic has no parallel in our modern history. The word 'unprecedented' really doesn't capture how challenging it has been. It has been a defining moment which we will be dealing with for years and years to come. For many who work in healthcare it has been a year of feeling terrified and helpless. Patients deteriorating at an alarming speed and quantity with no idea how to treat or care. Staff had to step up to doing stuff they normally left to the specialists.

People are desperate to 'get back to normal' when perhaps some things will never return to normal. The world as we knew it at the end of 2019 is no more for so many. Some things will change forever. The toll of the COVID-19 global pandemic has brought increased recognition of risks to patients and staff. In the beginning new treatments came with greater risk of harm. The physical and psychological safety of health workers was widely compromised, together with the capacity and financial stability of healthcare delivery systems. Situational factors, such as staffing shortages, staff redeployment to unfamiliar roles, and 'workarounds', all disrupted existing care processes in most health systems worldwide. The indirect effects of the virus on access to care have emerged as another form of harm. Delays have increased, patients have not sought treatment due to fear, people have been unable to physically go to health facilities because of lockdowns, or shielding, and those with complex chronic conditions have been in some respects in hiding for over two years.

What is clear is that the spread of infectious diseases knows no boundaries and has a unique ability to fuel fear, anxiety, and mass hysteria. We all feel completely out of control. The worst part of it is the invisibility of the enemy, the complete unknown about whether it is around you or on the surfaces you are touching or the people you are sitting next to.

With regard to the staff, most of them have worked at the very edge of their ability and safety. Not their capability but their ability to cope with the stress, exhaustion, overwhelming sense of guilt of not being able to provide the care they would like to provide. Staff have been exposed to experiences that have taken them to their limits. They are now suffering anxiety, depression, post-traumatic stress disorder, and burnout. These will significantly increase the risk of errors, incidents, and things not going to plan.

Roepe L. Rabasca published in July 2021 research about why workplace harassment and bullying, especially for people of different, gender, race, or ethnicity, increased during the pandemic. The research cited the changes in the way we communicate and our working environments, more one-to-one communication occurring in isolation, lines between work and home environments being blurred, and people acting or speaking in ways that are much more casual and informal that they normally would.

In September 2020, the theme for the World Patient Safety Day was 'Health Worker Safety: A Priority for Patient Safety'. The year of the pandemic has reinforced this in terms of the intensely difficult physical and psychological working conditions that staff have had to work with. The effects were everywhere, at work and at home. Staff were leaving their loved ones to stay elsewhere so as not to risk the spread. Heart-breaking decisions were made on a daily basis. The links between staff safety and patient safety have been starkly shown with both staff and patients at risk of infecting one another with COVID-19 together with the emotional and psychological hurt that the pandemic has caused to both patients and staff. The pandemic has really shone a light on safety in a very real and tangible way. The importance of health worker safety with regard to patient safety, particularly in the context of fatigue, stress, and personal protective equipment shortages, and rapid team formation and the risks thereof including psychological safety.

If we think about the pandemic, we can see that our healthcare systems were pushed further than ever before. People worked long hours to help victims at a potential cost to themselves. What we saw was resilience, self-organisation, and a reduction in hierarchy. However, there is only so much bounce back that people can do, the ability to recover has also been stretched beyond anything people have experienced before. There are always limits to resilience. Compassion helps us become resilient: it improves our immune response, reduces our stress levels, and is associated with the pleasure networks in our brains. One way to practise compassion is to ask a colleague, 'What's on your mind and how can I help?'

Safety has been impacted by the constant level of anxiety which has also affected our decisions, the sleep deprivation which makes us make mistakes, more anxious, and less safe. At the same time the staff are a vital source of information about how the system is functioning or not. This information could be used to predict failure rather than wait for the failure to occur. Effective clinical risk should be doing this. The tool for understanding the risks within your organisation is your staff.

The pandemic is one of those things that is a case study in complexity and complexity thinking. It is also a case study on preparedness or not and the gap between what we think we need (or what we imagine) and what we actually need. In terms of the response to the pandemic, there are many aspects that have reflected complexity thinking. The need for expertise, modelling, probability thinking, diverse perspectives. The need to respond to the unintended emergent consequences and the constant adaptations. The need to interact with people in different ways and make very quick decisions. The pandemic has led to a lot of people and resources being redeployed as required in an adaptive way, such as moving junior doctors from medical specialities with a lot of elective work to intensive care or acute medicine.

The ongoing impact on healthcare around the world will become clearer and fully quantified over time. However, important safety implications have emerged, with a heightened impetus to efforts that promote safer care at every level. Initial uncertainty has shifted to a growing understanding of the COVID-19 virus and its manifestations.

The COVID-19 pandemic has provided us all with a fast-tracked degree in infection, prevention, and control. People are using in their everyday language acronyms like PPE and terms like oxygen saturations, as well as really understanding about the importance of physical distancing, hand washing, and mask wearing. Suddenly the world of infection, prevention, and control became everyone's business, and not just on a need to know – everyone needed to be an expert. People were aghast about what they considered acceptable practices before the pandemic, such as intubation of patients without proper PPE.

Alongside the challenges, therefore, there have been some good things that have happened. The pandemic has also been characterised by rapid, real-time learning and responsiveness to new information and by dramatic changes to the way healthcare is delivered. Resources have been re-routed to the most urgent areas and face-to-face non-urgent work has been minimised so as to reduce viral transmission. Non-emergency operations have been cancelled or postponed, staff have been redeployed to acute medicine and ITU, and ITU capacity has been created by converting non-ITU areas (e.g., theatre recovery rooms).

The NHS has responded with incredible flexibility and dynamism. Staff were helped to get to work more easily by rescinding parking charges, being provided accommodation near the hospital. The focus on well-being in the workplace increased and there was an attempt to create a balanced and flexible day with the move from face-to-face or in-person work to online virtual activities. New technologies such as outpatient appointments delivered via telephone or video call, telephone triage, and video consultation increased with many wanting this to continue. Some have said that leadership support for frontline staff increased with a feeling of genuine engagement and listening and helping cut through the bottle necks or ineffective decision-making processes. Staff have felt able to take the initiative. Regular staff gatherings such as huddles or briefings increased which provided a stronger cohesive team.

With people having experienced an element of self-organisation they have enjoyed a whole new way of doing things. There has been a feeling of freedom and experimentation, and of course a certain amount of disorder. The conditions that encourage self-organisation often can be scary for individuals and threatening to power structures. People do not want to go back to the amount of bureaucracy they had before; they want to move away from the things they were doing that were time wasting and unnecessary.

As Dekker and Conklin (2022) suggest, maybe now is the time to de-clutter our systems. Everyone loves a clear out, everyone loves to see us remove things we don't need to do any more. There is such a huge amount of compliance and bureaucracy within healthcare and safety that de-cluttering could be really cathartic. More importantly it may help us work safer. Look at everything you measure, everything you collect, review your incident reporting systems, the way in which the policies are written and the systems we have designed. Study this with a view to reducing their complexity, reducing them in number, and making everything much clearer.

An understanding of complexity thinking would help navigate through the ongoing challenges the pandemic poses, including the ongoing vaccination programme, the impact of 'long COVID', and the now very long waiting lists. In an ideal world we would use everything we have learnt during the pandemic to make positive changes to our roles, workplaces, and activities. Shifting our places of work, interacting more digitally, addressing health and well-being for those that have worked in extraordinary conditions doing extraordinary hours and shifts. Jung is quoted as saying, 'In all disorder there is a secret order'. We need to get back to our secret order.

During the pandemic a lot of staff were call heroes or superheroes. The problem with calling healthcare staff heroes is that heroes are seen as infallible, able to deal with anything that comes their way, able to bounce back from any challenge. A hero is someone that has abilities far beyond ordinary people. While people who work in healthcare are talented, knowledgeable, and skilled they are still ordinary people. With the same flaws, the same ability to make mistakes, they are also not immune to the same feelings of fear, grief, shock, and anxiety. Healthcare workers are just ordinary human beings: who care, who feel, who make mistakes, and deserve to be treated as such.

Conclusion

The approach we have taken for the past two decades has been coined as safety-I. Safety-I focuses on understanding why an incident occurred using methods such as incident reporting, root cause analysis, failure modes and effects analysis, and so on. These have been adopted and sometimes adapted for use in healthcare from other high-risk industries such as aviation and air traffic control. We have concentrated the vast majority of our safety resources in this area and assumed that there is a linear causality and an individual culpability that can be understood and addressed. Safety-II focuses on what has gone right recognising that systems are complex and that humans are the solution not the problem.

There have been far less advances than we had hoped towards building safer systems since the publication of *an organisation with a memory*, which launched our safety movement in the UK. The problem with safety-I is that we are simply learning from the small number of times things fail. Safety-II learning comes from understanding individual and contextual factors within the complex adaptive system. The key question is whether safety-II will finally achieve the advances we are seeking.

There are concerns that without a change in perception, safety-II will end up with the same problems as safety-I simply because a safety-I mindset will be applied. To avoid this, we need to reconsider our approach, not just shift our approach. Instead of those working in safety learning on the job or alongside their day job of medicine, nursing, or administration. While these are a passionate hardworking group, there is a need for a recognition of the safety specialist as a distinct role with distinct skills and expertise from a formal training in safety science. Not as an add-on, but a role in its own right. These skills need to be not only for safety-II methodology but also for safety-I. For too long now people who have conducted some really important aspect of safety such as an investigation have done so with very little expert training. Research has shown that a large number of root cause analysis investigations failed to have any sustainable recommendations and have led to very few improvements. Not only is this a waste of resources it is hugely frustrating and in fact may be making the safety of patient care even worse.

It is early days with a few exploring how this new way of looking at safety can be applied. There is a need for a common understanding, a set of skills and tools as well as increased knowledge. Spread will require the development of safety-II tools to add to the safety-II tools. It also needs a safety-II mindset when using the safety-I tools. The latest iteration of the serious incident framework – the *patient safety incident response framework* – together with patient safety specialists and a patient safety curriculum go a long way to helping. But change will be slow unless we transform the work of safety into a profession, one with academic rigour, one that is respected.

Safety science includes ergonomics, human factors engineering, psychology, behavioural insights, sociology, and anthropology, to name a few. Applying the science of these fields to the complex adaptive system that is healthcare requires specialist knowledge and skills. Transforming what we do into a profession with a recognised qualification that is not simply a three-month training programme and key place in the healthcare team will ensure that safety is recognised as a priority and visible for everyone to see.

Increasing our expertise in safety-II is for me what we need to do in the next two decades. By understanding how we do our daily work, how we get things right, working out what we need to continue and what need to stop will help. By actually working with people who are doing the job day in day out, we could find the key to finally improving the safety of patient care. Whatever we call it, the way we 'do safety' has to change because we are doing these hardworking, compassionate healthcare staff a disservice. Helping people work safely is our cause, transforming our approach to safety is our goal, the safety of patient care is the outcome.

Change happens through learning and when people are exposed to new ideas and new ways of thinking. I hope that this book provides you with much food for thought, and that you in turn will share the learning. The more individuals who are made aware of these ideas and philosophies, the more there will be a critical mass of people who will seek the change and ultimately make a difference to the safety system as a whole.

References

Card, A J (2016) The Problem with '5 Whys'. *BMJ Quality and Safety* 26(8). Accessed via https://qualitysafety.bmj.com/content /26/8/671.

Clark, T R (2020) *The 4 Stages of Psychological Safety*. Oakland, CA: Berrett-Koehler Publishers, Inc.

Conklin, T (2020) *When the Worst Accident Happens: A Field Guide to Creating a Restorative Response to Workplace Fatalities and Catastrophic Events*. Santa Fe, NM: PreAccident Media.

Cook, R I (1998) How Complex Systems Fail (Being a Short Treatise on the Nature of Failure; How Failure is Evaluated; How Failure is Attributed to Proximate Cause; and the Resulting New Understanding of Patient Safety). Cognitive Technologies Laboratory, University of Chicago

Dekker, S (2018) *Just Culture: Restoring Trust and Accountability in Your Organisation*, 3rd edition. Boca Raton, FL: CRC Press.

Dekker, S, and Conklin, T (2022) *Do Safety Differently*. Santa Fe, NM: PreAccident Media.

Department of Health (2000) *An Organisation with a Memory*. London: The Stationery Office. Accessed via http://www.doh .gov.uk/pdfs/org.pdf.

Dixon-Woods, M, Leslie, M, Tarrant, C, and Bion, J (2013) Explaining Matching Michigan: An Ethnographic Study of a Patient Safety Program. *Implementation Science* 8(1): 70.

Edmondson, A C (2018) *The Fearless Organisation*. NJ, Hoboken: Wiley and Sons.

Hollnagel, E (2014) *Safety-I and Safety-II: The Past and Future of Safety Management*. Farnham: Ashgate.

Hollnagel, E, Wears, R L, and Braithwaite, J (2015) From Safety-I to Safety-II: A White Paper. *The Resilience Health Care Net.* Accessed 14 March 2022. http://resilienthealthcare.net/oneweb-media/WhitePaperFinal.pdf.

Iedema, R, Carroll, K, Collier, A, Hor, S, Mesman, J, and Wyer, M (2019) *Video-Reflexive Ethnography in Health Research and Healthcare Improvement: Theory and Application.* Boca Raton, FL: CRC Press.

Kahneman, D (2011) *Thinking, Fast and Slow.* Penguin.

Korstjens, I, Mesman, J, DeVries, R, and Nieuwehuizen, M. (2021) The Paradoxes of Communication and Collaboration in Maternity Care: A Video-Reflexivity Study with Professionals and Parents. *Women and Birth* 34(2): 145–153. https://doi.org/10.1016/j.wombi.2020.01.014.

Leape, L L (2021) *Making Healthcare Safe.* Springer International Publishing.

Lingard, L (2021) *The Question of Competence (The Culture and Politics of Health Care Work).* Ithaca, NY: Cornell University Press.

Macrae, C (2016) The Problem with Incident Reporting. *BMJ Quality and Safety* 25(2): 71–75. https://doi.org/10.1136/bmjqs-2015-004732.

Norman, D A (1988) *The Design of Everyday Things.* New York: Basic Books.

Project Aristotle (2016) *Information Guide.* Accessed via https://rework.withgoogle.com/print/guides/5721312655835136/.

Rabasca, R L (2021) Why Workplace Harassment Increased during the Pandemic. *Fast Company.* Accessed via https://www.fastcompany.com/90655155/why-workplace-harassment-increased-during-the-pandemic.

Reason, J (1990) *Human Error.* Cambridge: Cambridge University Press.

Rogers, E (2003) *Diffusion of Innovations,* 5th edition. Simon and Schuster. ISBN 978-0-7432-5823-4.

Seven Steps to Patient Safety (2003) accessed via http://www.wales.nhs.uk/documents/Sevenstepsoverview.pdf.

Shorrock, S (2022) accessed via www.humanisticsystems.com.

Vincent, C, Neale, G, and Woloshynowych, M (2001) Adverse Events in British Hospitals: Preliminary Retrospective Record Review. *British Medical Journal* 322(7285): 517–519.

Vincent, C A, and Amalberti, R (2016) *Safer Healthcare: Strategies for the Real World*. New York: Springer International.

Weick, K, and Sutcliffe, K (2007) *Managing Unexpected: Resilient Performance in Age of Uncertainty*. San Francisco, CA: John Wiley & Sons.

Zinck Pedersen, K, and Mesman, J (2021) A Transactional Approach to Patient Safety: Understanding Safe Care as a Collaborative Accomplishment. *Journal of Interprofessional Care*. http://doi.org/10.1080/13561820.2021.1874317.

Index

A

Accident and emergency (A&E)
    departments, 12
Accident causality model, 67
A&E, *see* Accident and emergency
    departments
Anecdotal evidence, 29
Anesthesia Patient Safety
    Foundation (APSF), 41
Australian Patient Safety
    Foundation, 41
Automaticity theorists, 39
Automatic thought processes, 39

B

Bandwagon effect, 71
Blame culture, 47

C

Care Quality Commission
    (CQC), 36
Catastrophe, 65
Catastrophic failure, 66
Causality, 69
Challenger safety, 134

Change management, 143
    components, 143
    factors affecting success, 144–145
Changing the culture, 119
Civility Saves Lives, 118
Clean Your Hands campaign, 50, 51
Clinical risk and regulation, 35–40
    adverse events, 42–46
    healthcare research, patient
        harm, 40–42
Clinicians, 53–54
Clostridium difficile (infection), 59
Coaching, 4
Collective competence, 30, 31, 34
Communication improvement, 136
Compassion, 130
Complex adaptive system, 11, 20,
    34, 93–101
    successful outcomes, 67
Complexity models, 97
Complex system, 94
Complicated system, 94
Confirmation bias, 71
Continued influence effect, 71
Contributor safety, 134
Contributory factors, 67
Correlation, 69
COVID-19, learning from, 149

complexity thinking, 154–155
effective clinical risk, 152
health worker safety, 151–152
heart-breaking decisions, 151
indirect effects of virus, 150
ongoing impact on
    healthcare, 153
situational factors, 150
staff gatherings, 154
technologies, 154
CQC, *see* Care Quality Commission
Critical care, reducing harm, 52
Culture
    components, 119
    ideas, 118
    literature on, 118
Culture of mediocrity, 56

D

Defensive attribution hypothesis, 72
Depersonalisation, 148
Deterioration, reducing harm, 52
Diffusion of innovations, 145

E

'Easy to see' incidents, 56
Effortful thought processes, 39
Emotional exhaustion, 148
Erroneous/unintentional
    workaround, 17
Ethnography, 11
Expertise, 32–33
Explicit knowledge, 39

F

Fishbowls, 140
5 whys technique, 63–64
    problem, 64–65
Formalised huddles, 138
Framing effect, 71

G

Global Action on Patient Safety, 74
Global Patient Safety Challenges, 72
Group attribution error, 71

H

Harvard Medical Practice Study, 45
Health and Social Care Act 2012, 75
Healthcare, 4, 7, 93; *see also*
    Individual entries
    after-event duty of care, 29
    balance of probabilities and
        risk, 22
    caring for people that care, 147–149
    complex adaptive system, 31
    field of human factors, 6
    interventions, 52
    staff training, 30
    teams, 33–35
    workers, 10
Heinrich's triangle, 61–62
High-reliability systems, 99
    characteristics, 99–100
High-risk medicines, 52
Hindsight bias, 71
Huddles, 137
    types, 138
Human errors, 19, 40, 60
    'with good intent,' 19
Human factors, 90–93

I

IHI, *see* Institute for Healthcare
    Improvement
Illusory truth effect, 71
Imagining things, 9
Implementation, 147
    principle, 53
    relationships, 147
Incident investigation, 65–69

Incident reporting systems, 54–60
  measuring safety in organisation,
    60–61
Incidents, 29
  analysis, 61–65
Incivility impact, 117–118
Inclusion safety, 132–133
Individualism in healthcare, 34
Information capturing huddles, 138
'In hindsight,' 24
Innocuous failures, 66
Institute for Healthcare
    Improvement (IHI), 52
Investigations, 120–121
Investigators, 67

J

Judgement, 16
Just world hypothesis, 72

L

Language in patient safety, 113–116
Leadership for safety, 52
Leadership intervention, 52, 53
Learner safety, 133
Learning from excellence, 111–113
Linear thinking, 96

M

Making Healthcare Safe, 75–76
Matching Michigan, 51
Medicines and Healthcare Products
    Regulatory Agency
    (MHRA), 36

N

Naïve realism, 70
National Health Service (NHS), xiv,
    36, 46, 47

learning from incidents, 48
  Sign Up to Safety (*see* Sign Up to
    Safety)
  to support safety improvement,
    81–83
National Patient Safety Agency
    (NPSA), 49, 50, 54, 75
  clinical reviewers, analysing
    incidents, 55
National Patient Safety
    Foundation, 49
National Public Radio (NPR), 28
The National Reporting and
    Learning System (NRLS),
    49, 53, 54, 81
National risk management
    system, 54
Negativity, 1
  negative feedback, 2–3
  problem with getting caught up, 2
  unequal learning, 3
Neglect of probability, 70
Never events, 20
NHS, *see* National Health Service
NHS Litigation Authority (NHSLA),
    35, 37, 54
'No blame' culture, 121, 122
NPSA, *see* National Patient Safety
    Agency
NRLS, *see* National Reporting and
    Learning System

O

Omission bias, 70
'One minute silence technique,' 142
'One new step,' 53
'One size fits all' approach, 84
Operation Life, 52
Optimising workaround, 17
Organisational culture, 47–48
An Organisation with a Memory,
    46, 47, 49

organisational culture, 47–48
reporting systems, 48
Outcome bias, 70
Overconfidence effect, 70

P

Paediatric intensive care, 23
case study, 25–27
Patient Safety First, 52, 77
Patient Safety First Week, 53
Patient Safety Incident Response
Framework, 81, 158
Performing work, 6
Perioperative care, reducing harm, 52
Permanence, 27
Personal competence, 30
Personalisation, 27
anecdotal evidence, 29
aspect of, 30
collective competence, 31
people living with guilt and
shame, case study, 27–29
personal competence, 30
Pervasiveness, 27
Preventability, 46
Psychological safety, 127–131, 147
sequential stages, 131
challenger safety, 134
contributor safety, 134
inclusion safety, 132–133
learner safety, 133
'Punaha ahuru' commission, 105

Q

Quantitative measures, 12

R

RCA, *see* Root cause analysis
Reflexivity, 11

Relationships, 147
Reporting systems, 48
Reproducibility, 108
Restorative just culture, 115–116,
124, 125
'no blame' culture, 121, 122
Restorative justice, 126
Retrospective case notes
reviews, 45
Risk management system, 25
Risk resilience, 89
components, 90
key elements, 89
Root cause analysis (RCA),
63–67, 121
Routine cases/times of boredom, 39
Routine workaround, 17

S

Safer Healthcare Now, 52
Safer Patients Initiative, 52
Safety culture, 119
essentials, 119–120
talking to each other, 134
Safety-I, 157
attitude to error, 18–22
biases, 70–72
defined, 1
healthcare systems, 9
policies and procedures, 4–6
problem, 157
vs. Safety-II, 103–105
Safety-II approach, 11, 87–89
action points to support
healthcare workers,
109–111
complex adaptive systems,
93–101
human factors, 90–93
learning from excellence,
111–113, 157

list things from theory, 105–106
ordinary aspects of healthcare,
     106–108
problem with language, 113–116
risk resilience, 89–90
strategy implementation, 83–84
ways to improve
     communication, 136
Safety incidents, 98
Safety movement, 85
Safety myths, 22–23
Safety science, 158
Safety Surgery Saves Lives
     initiative, 72
  surgical checklist, 72
    barriers hindering
       implementation, 74
    testing, 73–74
    three stages, 72–73
Schwartz Rounds, 136–142
Science of safety, 48
Seven Steps to Patient Safety, 50
Sign Up to Safety, 76
  adapting to rhythm of
     change, 80
  creating brand, 79, 80
  key lessons, 77, 80–81
  Patient Safety First, 77
  philosophy of local
     ownership, 79
  social movement theory, 78
  strategic aims to support
     development, 81
Silence, 142
Simple linear accident models, 97
Situational awareness, 91, 92
Situational/exceptional
     workaround, 17
Social movements, 80
Social movement theory, 78
Still Not Safe, 84–86
Stretch goals, 22

Successful outcomes, 67
Swiss cheese model, 62–63
Systems thinking, 38, 92

T

Tacit knowledge, 39
Teaming, 34
Teamwork, 33–35
Traditional linear thinking, 97
Training on safety, 33
Trio-conversations, 139
Trios, 139

U

Ultra-adaptive systems, 98–99
Ultra-safe healthcare system, 34
Ultra-safe systems, 100–101
Unequal learning, 3
Unplanned impromptu
     huddles, 138
Unprecedented, 150
Unsupported health workers, 29

V

Video reflexive ethnography (VRE),
     107, 109
Video reflexivity, 107, 108
  methodology, 11
Vincent study, 46
Violations, 5
VRE, *see* Video reflexive
     ethnography

W

WHA, *see* World Health Assembly
WHO, *see* World Health
     Organization
'Wisdom of the crowd,' 71

Workarounds, 16
   paediatric intensive care, 23
   types, 17
Work-as-analysed, 12, 15
Work-as-disclosed, 13, 16
   partial truth, 15
Work-as-done, 7, 8, 16, 24, 88
   degree of fatigue, 8
Work-as-imagined, 8, 15
Work-as-instructed, 10, 15
Work-as-judged, 12, 15, 69
Work-as-measured, 11, 12, 15
Work-as-observed, 10, 15
   ethnographic study, 11
Work-as-prescribed, 9, 15
   judgement, 16
Work as simulated, 12, 13

'Working safely,' 116
World Alliance for Patient Safety, 72
World Café, 137
World Health Assembly (WHA), 74
World Health Organisation Global
   Safety Challenges, 52
World Health Organization (WHO),
   21, 72, 75
   seven guiding principles, 75
World Patient Safety Day, 21, 151

Z

Zero harm, 20
   actions to achieve, 21
   myth of, 22
   principle, 20